AI Self-Driving Cars Breakthroughs

Practical Advances in
Artificial Intelligence and Machine Learning

Dr. Lance B. Eliot, MBA, PhD

DEDICATION

To my incredible son, Michael, and my incredible daughter, Lauren.

Forest fortuna adiuvat (from the Latin; good fortune favors the brave).

CONTENTS

Lance B. Eliot

ACKNOWLEDGMENTS

I have been the beneficiary of advice and counsel by many friends, colleagues, family, investors, and many others. I want to thank everyone that has aided me throughout my career. I write from the heart and the head, having experienced first-hand what it means to have others around you that support you during the good times and the tough times.

To Warren Bennis, one of my doctoral advisors and ultimately a colleague, I offer my deepest thanks and appreciation, especially for his calm and insightful wisdom and support.

To Mark Stevens and his generous efforts toward funding and supporting the USC Stevens Center for Innovation.

To Lloyd Greif and the USC Lloyd Greif Center for Entrepreneurial Studies for their ongoing encouragement of founders and entrepreneurs.

To Peter Drucker, William Wang, Aaron Levie, Peter Kim, Jon Kraft, Cindy Crawford, Jenny Ming, Steve Milligan, Chis Underwood, Frank Gehry, Buzz Aldrin, Steve Forbes, Bill Thompson, Dave Dillon, Alan Fuerstman, Larry Ellison, Jim Sinegal, John Sperling, Mark Stevenson, Anand Nallathambi, Thomas Barrack, Jr., and many other innovators and leaders that I have met and gained mightily from doing so.

Thanks to Ed Trainor, Kevin Anderson, James Hickey, Wendell Jones, Ken Harris, DuWayne Peterson, Mike Brown, Jim Thornton, Abhi Beniwal, Al Biland, John Nomura, Eliot Weinman, John Desmond, and many others for their unwavering support during my career.

And most of all thanks as always to Michael and Lauren, for their ongoing support and for having seen me writing and heard much of this material during the many months involved in writing it. To their patience and willingness to listen.

INTRODUCTION

This is a book that provides the newest innovations and the latest Artificial Intelligence (AI) advances about the emerging nature of AI-based autonomous self-driving driverless cars. Via recent advances in Artificial Intelligence (AI) and Machine Learning (ML), we are nearing the day when vehicles can control themselves and will not require and nor rely upon human intervention to perform their driving tasks (or, that <u>allow</u> for human intervention, but only *require* human intervention in very limited ways).

Similar to my other related books, which I describe in a moment and list the chapters in the Appendix A of this book, I am particularly focused on those advances that pertain to self-driving cars. The phrase "autonomous vehicles" is often used to refer to any kind of vehicle, whether it is ground-based or in the air or sea, and whether it is a cargo hauling trailer truck or a conventional passenger car. Though the aspects described in this book are certainly applicable to all kinds of autonomous vehicles, I am focused more so here on cars.

Indeed, I am especially known for my role in aiding the advancement of self-driving cars, serving currently as the Executive Director of the Cybernetic Self-Driving Cars Institute.. In addition to writing software, designing and developing systems and software for self-driving cars, I also speak and write quite a bit about the topic. This book is a collection of some of my more advanced essays. For those of you that might have seen my essays posted elsewhere, I have updated them and integrated them into this book as one handy cohesive package.

You might be interested in companion books that I have written that provide additional key innovations and fundamentals about self-driving cars. Those books are entitled **"Introduction to Driverless Self-Driving Cars," "Advances in AI and Autonomous Vehicles: Cybernetic Self-Driving Cars," "Self-Driving Cars: "The Mother of All AI Projects," "Innovation and Thought Leadership on Self-Driving Driverless Cars," "New Advances in AI Autonomous Driverless Self-Driving Cars," and "Autonomous Vehicle Driverless Self-Driving Cars and**

1

Artificial Intelligence," "Transformative Artificial Intelligence Driverless Self-Driving Cars," "Disruptive Artificial Intelligence and Driverless Self-Driving Cars, and "State-of-the-Art AI Driverless Self-Driving Cars," and "Top Trends in AI Self-Driving Cars," and "AI Innovations and Self-Driving Cars," "Crucial Advances for AI Driverless Cars," "Sociotechnical Insights and AI Driverless Cars," "Pioneering Advances for AI Driverless Cars" and "Leading Edge Trends for AI Driverless Cars," "The Cutting Edge of AI Autonomous Cars" and "The Next Wave of AI Self-Driving Cars" and "Revolutionary Innovations of AI Self-Driving Cars," and "AI Self-Driving Cars Breakthroughs" (they are all available via Amazon). See Appendix A of this herein book to see a listing of the chapters covered in those three books.

For the introduction here to this book, I am going to borrow my introduction from those companion books, since it does a good job of laying out the landscape of self-driving cars and my overall viewpoints on the topic. The remainder of the book is all new material that does not appear in the companion books.

INTRODUCTION TO SELF-DRIVING CARS

This is a book about self-driving cars. Someday in the future, we'll all have self-driving cars and this book will perhaps seem antiquated, but right now, we are at the forefront of the self-driving car wave. Daily news bombards us with flashes of new announcements by one car maker or another and leaves the impression that within the next few weeks or maybe months that the self-driving car will be here. A casual non-technical reader would assume from these news flashes that in fact we must be on the cusp of a true self-driving car.

Here's a real news flash: We are still quite a distance from having a true self-driving car. It is years to go before we get there.

Why is that? Because a true self-driving car is akin to a moonshot. In the same manner that getting us to the moon was an incredible feat, likewise can it be said for achieving a true self-driving car. Anybody that suggests or even brashly states that the true self-driving car is nearly here should be viewed with great skepticism. Indeed, you'll see that I often tend to use the word "hogwash" or "crock" when I assess much of the decidedly *fake news* about self-driving cars. Those of us on the inside know that what is often reported to the outside is malarkey. Few of the insiders are willing to say so. I have no such hesitation.

Indeed, I've been writing a popular blog post about self-driving cars and hitting hard on those that try to wave their hands and pretend that we are on the imminent verge of true self-driving cars. For many years, I've been known as the AI Insider. Besides writing about AI, I also develop AI software. I do what I describe. It also gives me insights into what others that are doing AI are really doing versus what it is said they are doing.

Many faithful readers had asked me to pull together my insightful short essays and put them into another book, which you are now holding in your hands.

For those of you that have been reading my essays over the years, this collection not only puts them together into one handy package, I also updated the essays and added new material. For those of you that are new to the topic of self-driving cars and AI, I hope you find these essays approachable and informative. I also tend to have a writing style with a bit of a voice, and so you'll see that I am times have a wry sense of humor and poke at conformity.

As a former professor and founder of an AI research lab, I for many years wrote in the formal language of academic writing. I published in referred journals and served as an editor for several AI journals. This writing here is not of the nature, and I have adopted a different and more informal style for these essays. That being said, I also do mention from time-to-time more rigorous material on AI and encourage you all to dig into those deeper and more formal materials if so interested.

I am also an AI practitioner. This means that I write AI software for a living. Currently, I head-up the Cybernetics Self-Driving Car Institute, where we are developing AI software for self-driving cars. I am excited to also report that my son, also a software engineer, heads-up our Cybernetics Self-Driving Car Lab. What I have helped to start, and for which he is an integral part, ultimately he will carry long into the future after I have retired. My daughter, a marketing whiz, also is integral to our efforts as head of our Marketing group. She too will carry forward the legacy now being formulated.

For those of you that are reading this book and have a penchant for writing code, you might consider taking a look at the open source code available for self-driving cars. This is a handy place to start learning how to develop AI for self-driving cars. There are also many new educational courses spring forth.

There is a growing body of those wanting to learn about and develop self-driving cars, and a growing body of colleges, labs, and other avenues by which you can learn about self-driving cars.

This book will provide a foundation of aspects that I think will get you ready for those kinds of more advanced training opportunities. If you've already taken those classes, you'll likely find these essays especially interesting as they offer a perspective that I am betting few other instructors or faculty offered to you. These are challenging essays that ask you to think beyond the conventional about self-driving cars.

THE MOTHER OF ALL AI PROJECTS

In June 2017, Apple CEO Tim Cook came out and finally admitted that Apple has been working on a self-driving car. As you'll see in my essays, Apple was enmeshed in secrecy about their self-driving car efforts. We have only been able to read the tea leaves and guess at what Apple has been up to. The notion of an iCar has been floating for quite a while, and self-driving engineers and researchers have been signing tight-lipped Non-Disclosure Agreements (NDA's) to work on projects at Apple that were as shrouded in mystery as any military invasion plans might be.

Tim Cook said something that many others in the Artificial Intelligence (AI) field have been saying, namely, the creation of a self-driving car has got to be the mother of all AI projects. In other words, it is in fact a tremendous moonshot for AI. If a self-driving car can be crafted and the AI works as we hope, it means that we have made incredible strides with AI and that therefore it opens many other worlds of potential breakthrough accomplishments that AI can solve.

Is this hyperbole? Am I just trying to make AI seem like a miracle worker and so provide self-aggrandizing statements for those of us writing the AI software for self-driving cars? No, it is not hyperbole. Developing a true self-driving car is really, really, really hard to do. Let me take a moment to explain why. As a side note, I realize that the Apple CEO is known for at times uttering hyperbole, and he had previously said for example that the year 2012 was "the mother of all years," and he had said that the release of iOS 10 was "the mother of all releases" – all of which does suggest he likes to use the handy "mother of" expression. But, I assure you, in terms of true self-driving cars, he has hit the nail on the head. For sure.

When you think about a moonshot and how we got to the moon, there are some identifiable characteristics and those same aspects can be applied to creating a true self-driving car. You'll notice that I keep putting the word "true" in front of the self-driving car expression. I do so because as per my essay about the various levels of self-driving cars, there are some self-driving cars that are only somewhat of a self-driving car. The somewhat versions are ones that require a human driver to be ready to intervene. In my view, that's not a true self-driving car. A true self-driving car is one that requires no human driver intervention at all. It is a car that can entirely undertake via automation the driving task without any human driver needed. This is the essence of what is known as a Level 5 self-driving car. We are currently at the Level 2 and Level 3 mark, and not yet at Level 5.

Getting to the moon involved aspects such as having big stretch goals, incremental progress, experimentation, innovation, and so on. Let's review how this applied to the moonshot of the bygone era, and how it applies to the self-driving car moonshot of today.

Big Stretch Goal

Trying to take a human and deliver the human to the moon, and bring them back, safely, was an extremely large stretch goal at the time. No one knew whether it could be done. The technology wasn't available yet. The cost was huge. The determination would need to be fierce. Etc. To reach a Level 5 self-driving car is going to be the same. It is a big stretch goal. We can readily get to the Level 3, and we are able to see the Level 4 just up ahead, but a Level 5 is still an unknown as to if it is doable. It should eventually be doable and in the same way that we thought we'd eventually get to the moon, but when it will occur is a different story.

Incremental Progress

Getting to the moon did not happen overnight in one fell swoop. It took years and years of incremental progress to get there. Likewise for self-driving cars. Google has famously been striving to get to the Level 5, and pretty much been willing to forgo dealing with the intervening levels, but most of the other self-driving car makers are doing the incremental route. Let's get a good Level 2 and a somewhat Level 3 going. Then, let's improve the Level 3 and get a somewhat Level 4 going. Then, let's improve the Level 4 and finally arrive at a Level 5. This seems to be the prevalent way that we are going to achieve the true self-driving car.

Experimentation

You likely know that there were various experiments involved in perfecting the approach and technology to get to the moon. As per making incremental progress, we first tried to see if we could get a rocket to go into space and safety return, then put a monkey in there, then with a human, then we went all the way to the moon but didn't land, and finally we arrived at the mission that actually landed on the moon. Self-driving cars are the same way. We are doing simulations of self-driving cars. We do testing of self-driving cars on private land under controlled situations. We do testing of self-driving cars on public roadways, often having to meet regulatory requirements including for example having an engineer or equivalent in the car to take over the controls if needed. And so on. Experiments big and small are needed to figure out what works and what doesn't.

Innovation

There are already some advances in AI that are allowing us to progress toward self-driving cars. We are going to need even more advances. Innovation in all aspects of technology are going to be required to achieve a true self-driving car. By no means do we already have everything in-hand that we need to get there. Expect new inventions and new approaches, new algorithms, etc.

Setbacks

Most of the pundits are avoiding talking about potential setbacks in the progress toward self-driving cars. Getting to the moon involved many setbacks, some of which you never have heard of and were buried at the time so as to not dampen enthusiasm and funding for getting to the moon. A recurring theme in many of my included essays is that there are going to be setbacks as we try to arrive at a true self-driving car. Take a deep breath and be ready. I just hope the setbacks don't completely stop progress. I am sure that it will cause progress to alter in a manner that we've not yet seen in the self-driving car field. I liken the self-driving car of today to the excitement everyone had for Uber when it first got going. Today, we have a different view of Uber and with each passing day there are more regulations to the ride sharing business and more concerns raised. The darling child only stays a darling until finally that child acts up. It will happen the same with self-driving cars.

SELF-DRIVING CARS CHALLENGES

But what exactly makes things so hard to have a true self-driving car, you might be asking. You have seen cruise control for years and years. You've lately seen cars that can do parallel parking. You've seen YouTube videos of Tesla drivers that put their hands out the window as their car zooms along the highway, and seen to therefore be in a self-driving car. Aren't we just needing to put a few more sensors onto a car and then we'll have in-hand a true self-driving car? Nope.

Consider for a moment the nature of the driving task. We don't just let anyone at any age drive a car. Worldwide, most countries won't license a driver until the age of 18, though many do allow a learner's permit at the age of 15 or 16. Some suggest that a younger age would be physically too small to reach the controls of the car. Though this might be the case, we could easily adjust the controls to allow for younger aged and thus smaller stature. It's not their physical size that matters. It's their cognitive development that matters.

To drive a car, you need to be able to reason about the car, what the car can and cannot do. You need to know how to operate the car. You need to know about how other cars on the road drive. You need to know what is allowed in driving such as speed limits and driving within marked lanes. You need to be able to react to situations and be able to avoid getting into accidents. You need to ascertain when to hit your brakes, when to steer clear of a pedestrian, and how to keep from ramming that motorcyclist that just cut you off.

Many of us had taken courses on driving. We studied about driving and took driver training. We had to take a test and pass it to be able to drive. The point being that though most adults take the driving task for granted, and we often "mindlessly" drive our cars, there is a significant amount of cognitive effort that goes into driving a car. After a while, it becomes second nature. You don't especially think about how you drive, you just do it. But, if you watch a novice driver, say a teenager learning to drive, you suddenly realize that there is a lot more complexity to it than we seem to realize.

Furthermore, driving is a very serious task. I recall when my daughter and son first learned to drive. They are both very conscientious people. They wanted to make sure that whatever they did, they did well, and that they did not harm anyone. Every day, when you get into a car, it is probably around 4,000 pounds of hefty metal and plastics (about two tons), and it is a lethal weapon. Think about it. You drive down the street in an object that weighs two tons and with the engine it can accelerate and ram into anything you want to hit. The damage a car can inflict is very scary. Both my children were surprised that they were being given the right to maneuver this monster of a beast that could cause tremendous harm entirely by merely letting go of the steering wheel for a moment or taking your eyes off the road.

In fact, in the United States alone there are about 30,000 deaths per year by auto accidents, which is around 100 per day. Given that there are about 263 million cars in the United States, I am actually more amazed that the number of fatalities is not a lot higher. During my morning commute, I look at all the thousands of cars on the freeway around me, and I think that if all of them decided to go zombie and drive in a crazy maniac way, there would be many people dead. Somehow, incredibly, each day, most people drive relatively safely. To me, that's a miracle right there. Getting millions and millions of people to be safe and sane when behind the wheel of a two ton mobile object, it's a feat that we as a society should admire with pride.

So, hopefully you are in agreement that the driving task requires a great deal of cognition. You don't' need to be especially smart to drive a car, and we've done quite a bit to make car driving viable for even the average dolt. There isn't an IQ test that you need to take to drive a car. If you can read and write, and pass a test, you pretty much can legally drive a car. There are of course some that drive a car and are not legally permitted to do so, plus there are private areas such as farms where drivers are young, but for public roadways in the United States, you can be generally of average intelligence (or less) and be able to legally drive.

This though makes it seem like the cognitive effort must not be much. If the cognitive effort was truly hard, wouldn't we only have Einstein's that could drive a car? We have made sure to keep the driving task as simple as we can, by making the controls easy and relatively standardized, and by having roads that are relatively standardized, and so on. It is as though Disneyland has put their Autopia into the real-world, by us all as a society agreeing that roads will be a certain way, and we'll all abide by the various rules of driving.

A modest cognitive task by a human is still something that stymies AI. You certainly know that AI has been able to beat chess players and be good at other kinds of games. This type of narrow cognition is not what car driving is about. Car driving is much wider. It requires knowledge about the world, which a chess playing AI system does not need to know. The cognitive aspects of driving are on the one hand seemingly simple, but at the same time require layer upon layer of knowledge about cars, people, roads, rules, and a myriad of other "common sense" aspects. We don't have any AI systems today that have that same kind of breadth and depth of awareness and knowledge.

As revealed in my essays, the self-driving car of today is using trickery to do particular tasks. It is all very narrow in operation. Plus, it currently assumes that a human driver is ready to intervene. It is like a child that we have taught to stack blocks, but we are needed to be right there in case the child stacks them too high and they begin to fall over. AI of today is brittle, it is narrow, and it does not approach the cognitive abilities of humans. This is why the true self-driving car is somewhere out in the future.

Another aspect to the driving task is that it is not solely a mind exercise. You do need to use your senses to drive. You use your eyes a vision sensors to see the road ahead. You vision capability is like a streaming video, which your brain needs to continually analyze as you drive. Where is the road? Is there a pedestrian in the way? Is there another car ahead of you? Your senses are relying a flood of info to your brain. Self-driving cars are trying to do the same, by using cameras, radar, ultrasound, and lasers. This is an attempt at mimicking how humans have senses and sensory apparatus.

Thus, the driving task is mental and physical. You use your senses, you use your arms and legs to manipulate the controls of the car, and you use your brain to assess the sensory info and direct your limbs to act upon the controls of the car. This all happens instantly. If you've ever perhaps gotten something in your eye and only had one eye available to drive with, you suddenly realize how dependent upon vision you are. If you have a broken foot with a cast, you suddenly realize how hard it is to control the brake pedal and the accelerator. If you've taken medication and your brain is maybe sluggish, you suddenly realize how much mental strain is required to drive a car.

An AI system that plays chess only needs to be focused on playing chess. The physical aspects aren't important because usually a human moves the chess pieces or the chessboard is shown on an electronic display. Using AI for a more life-and-death task such as analyzing MRI images of patients, this again does not require physical capabilities and instead is done by examining images of bits.

Driving a car is a true life-and-death task. It is a use of AI that can easily and at any moment produce death. For those colleagues of mine that are developing this AI, as am I, we need to keep in mind the somber aspects of this. We are producing software that will have in its virtual hands the lives of the occupants of the car, and the lives of those in other nearby cars, and the lives of nearby pedestrians, etc. Chess is not usually a life-or-death matter.

Driving is all around us. Cars are everywhere. Most of today's AI applications involve only a small number of people. Or, they are behind the scenes and we as humans have other recourse if the AI messes up. AI that is driving a car at 80 miles per hour on a highway had better not mess up. The consequences are grave. Multiply this by the number of cars, if we could put magically self-driving into every car in the USA, we'd have AI running in the 263 million cars. That's a lot of AI spread around. This is AI on a massive scale that we are not doing today and that offers both promise and potential peril.

There are some that want AI for self-driving cars because they envision a world without any car accidents. They envision a world in which there is no car congestion and all cars cooperate with each other. These are wonderful utopian visions.

They are also very misleading. The adoption of self-driving cars is going to be incremental and not overnight. We cannot economically just junk all existing cars. Nor are we going to be able to affordably retrofit existing cars. It is more likely that self-driving cars will be built into new cars and that over many years of gradual replacement of existing cars that we'll see the mix of self-driving cars become substantial in the real-world.

In these essays, I have tried to offer technological insights without being overly technical in my description, and also blended the business, societal, and economic aspects too. Technologists need to consider the non-technological impacts of what they do. Non-technologists should be aware of what is being developed.

We all need to work together to collectively be prepared for the enormous disruption and transformative aspects of true self-driving cars. We all need to be involved in this mother of all AI projects.

WHAT THIS BOOK PROVIDES

What does this book provide to you? It introduces many of the key elements about self-driving cars and does so with an AI based perspective. I weave together technical and non-technical aspects, readily going from being concerned about the cognitive capabilities of the driving task and how the technology is embodying this into self-driving cars, and in the next breath I discuss the societal and economic aspects.

They are all intertwined because that's the way reality is. You cannot separate out the technology per se, and instead must consider it within the milieu of what is being invented and innovated, and do so with a mindset towards the contemporary mores and culture that shape what we are doing and what we hope to do.

WHY THIS BOOK

I wrote this book to try and bring to the public view many aspects about self-driving cars that nobody seems to be discussing.

For business leaders that are either involved in making self-driving cars or that are going to leverage self-driving cars, I hope that this book will enlighten you as to the risks involved and ways in which you should be strategizing about how to deal with those risks.

For entrepreneurs, startups and other businesses that want to enter into the self-driving car market that is emerging, I hope this book sparks your interest in doing so, and provides some sense of what might be prudent to pursue.

For researchers that study self-driving cars, I hope this book spurs your interest in the risks and safety issues of self-driving cars, and also nudges you toward conducting research on those aspects.

For students in computer science or related disciplines, I hope this book will provide you with interesting and new ideas and material, for which you might conduct research or provide some career direction insights for you.

For AI companies and high-tech companies pursuing self-driving cars, this book will hopefully broaden your view beyond just the mere coding and development needed to make self-driving cars.

For all readers, I hope that you will find the material in this book to be stimulating. Some of it will be repetitive of things you already know. But I am pretty sure that you'll also find various eureka moments whereby you'll discover a new technique or approach that you had not earlier thought of. I am also betting that there will be material that forces you to rethink some of your current practices.

I am not saying you will suddenly have an epiphany and change what you are doing. I do think though that you will reconsider or perhaps revisit what you are doing.

For anyone choosing to use this book for teaching purposes, please take a look at my suggestions for doing so, as described in the Appendix. I have found the material handy in courses that I have taught, and likewise other faculty have told me that they have found the material handy, in some cases as extended readings and in other instances as a core part of their course (depending on the nature of the class).

In my writing for this book, I have tried carefully to blend both the practitioner and the academic styles of writing. It is not as dense as is typical academic journal writing, but at the same time offers depth by going into the nuances and trade-offs of various practices.

The word "deep" is in vogue today, meaning getting deeply into a subject or topic, and so is the word "unpack" which means to tease out the underlying aspects of a subject or topic. I have sought to offer material that addresses an issue or topic by going relatively deeply into it and make sure that it is well unpacked.

Finally, in any book about AI, it is difficult to use our everyday words without having some of them be misinterpreted. Specifically, it is easy to anthropomorphize AI. When I say that an AI system "knows" something, I do not want you to construe that the AI system has sentience and "knows" in the same way that humans do. They aren't that way, as yet. I have tried to use quotes around such words from time-to-time to emphasize that the words I am using should not be misinterpreted to ascribe true human intelligence to the AI systems that we know of today. If I used quotes around all such words, the book would be very difficult to read, and so I am doing so judiciously. Please keep that in mind as you read the material, thanks.

Lance B. Eliot

COMPANION BOOKS

If you find this material of interest, you might enjoy these too:

1. **"Introduction to Driverless Self-Driving Cars"** by Dr. Lance Eliot

2. **"Innovation and Thought Leadership on Self-Driving Driverless Cars"** by Dr. Lance Eliot

3. **"Advances in AI and Autonomous Vehicles: Cybernetic Self-Driving Cars"** by Dr. Lance Eliot

4. **"Self-Driving Cars: The Mother of All AI Projects"** by Dr. Lance Eliot

5. **"New Advances in AI Autonomous Driverless Self-Driving Cars"** by Dr. Lance Eliot

6. **"Autonomous Vehicle Driverless Self-Driving Cars and Artificial Intelligence"** by Dr. Lance Eliot and Michael B. Eliot

7. **"Transformative Artificial Intelligence Driverless Self-Driving Cars"** by Dr. Lance Eliot

8. **"Disruptive Artificial Intelligence and Driverless Self-Driving Cars"** by Dr. Lance Eliot

9. "State-of-the-Art AI Driverless Self-Driving Cars" by Dr. Lance Eliot

10. "Top Trends in AI Self-Driving Cars" by Dr. Lance Eliot

11. **"AI Innovations and Self-Driving Cars"** by Dr. Lance Eliot

12. **"Crucial Advances for AI Driverless Cars"** by Dr. Lance Eliot

13. **"Sociotechnical Insights and AI Driverless Cars"** by Dr. Lance Eliot.

14. **"Pioneering Advances for AI Driverless Cars"** by Dr. Lance Eliot

15. **"Leading Edge Trends for AI Driverless Cars"** by Dr. Lance Eliot

16. **"The Cutting Edge of AI Autonomous Cars"** by Dr. Lance Eliot

17. **"The Next Wave of AI Self-Driving Cars"** by Dr. Lance Eliot

18. **"Revolutionary Innovations of AI Driverless Cars"** by Dr. Lance Eliot

19. **"AI Self-Driving Cars Breakthroughs"** by Dr. Lance Eliot

All of the above books are available on Amazon and at other major global booksellers.

CHAPTER 1

ELIOT FRAMEWORK FOR AI SELF-DRIVING CARS

CHAPTER 1

ELIOT FRAMEWORK FOR
AI SELF-DRIVING CARS

This chapter is a core foundational aspect for understanding AI self-driving cars and I have used this same chapter in several of my other books to introduce the reader to essential elements of this field. Once you've read this chapter, you'll be prepared to read the rest of the material since the foundational essence of the components of autonomous AI driverless self-driving cars will have been established for you.

———

When I give presentations about self-driving cars and teach classes on the topic, I have found it helpful to provide a framework around which the various key elements of self-driving cars can be understood and organized (see diagram at the end of this chapter). The framework needs to be simple enough to convey the overarching elements, but at the same time not so simple that it belies the true complexity of self-driving cars. As such, I am going to describe the framework here and try to offer in a thousand words (or more!) what the framework diagram itself intends to portray.

The core elements on the diagram are numbered for ease of reference. The numbering does not suggest any kind of prioritization of the elements. Each element is crucial. Each element has a purpose, and otherwise would not be included in the framework. For some self-driving cars, a particular element might be more important or somehow distinguished in comparison to other self-driving cars.

You could even use the framework to rate a particular self-driving car, doing so by gauging how well it performs in each of the elements of the framework. I will describe each of the elements, one at a time. After doing so, I'll discuss aspects that illustrate how the elements interact and perform during the overall effort of a self-driving car.

At the Cybernetic Self-Driving Car Institute, we use the framework to keep track of what we are working on, and how we are developing software that fills in what is needed to achieve Level 5 self-driving cars.

D-01: Sensor Capture

Let's start with the one element that often gets the most attention in the press about self-driving cars, namely, the sensory devices for a self-driving car.

On the framework, the box labeled as D-01 indicates "Sensor Capture" and refers to the processes of the self-driving car that involve collecting data from the myriad of sensors that are used for a self-driving car. The types of devices typically involved are listed, such as the use of mono cameras, stereo cameras, LIDAR devices, radar systems, ultrasonic devices, GPS, IMU, and so on.

These devices are tasked with obtaining data about the status of the self-driving car and the world around it. Some of the devices are continually providing updates, while others of the devices await an indication by the self-driving car that the device is supposed to collect data. The data might be first transformed in some fashion by the device itself, or it might instead be fed directly into the sensor capture as raw data. At that point, it might be up to the sensor capture processes to do transformations on the data. This all varies depending upon the nature of the devices being used and how the devices were designed and developed.

D-02: Sensor Fusion

Imagine that your eyeballs receive visual images, your nose receives odors, your ears receive sounds, and in essence each of your distinct sensory devices is getting some form of input. The input befits the nature of the device. Likewise, for a self-driving car, the cameras provide visual images, the radar returns radar reflections, and so on.

Each device provides the data as befits what the device does.

At some point, using the analogy to humans, you need to merge together what your eyes see, what your nose smells, what your ears hear, and piece it all together into a larger sense of what the world is all about and what is happening around you. Sensor fusion is the action of taking the singular aspects from each of the devices and putting them together into a larger puzzle.

Sensor fusion is a tough task. There are some devices that might not be working at the time of the sensor capture. Or, there might some devices that are unable to report well what they have detected. Again, using a human analogy, suppose you are in a dark room and so your eyes cannot see much. At that point, you might need to rely more so on your ears and what you hear. The same is true for a self-driving car. If the cameras are obscured due to snow and sleet, it might be that the radar can provide a greater indication of what the external conditions consist of.

In the case of a self-driving car, there can be a plethora of such sensory devices. Each is reporting what it can. Each might have its difficulties. Each might have its limitations, such as how far ahead it can detect an object. All of these limitations need to be considered during the sensor fusion task.

D-03: Virtual World Model

For humans, we presumably keep in our minds a model of the world around us when we are driving a car. In your mind, you know that the car is going at say 60 miles per hour and that you are on a freeway. You have a model in your mind that your car is surrounded by other cars, and that there are lanes to the freeway. Your model is not only based on what you can see, hear, etc., but also what you know about the nature of the world. You know that at any moment that car ahead of you can smash on its brakes, or the car behind you can ram into your car, or that the truck in the next lane might swerve into your lane.

The AI of the self-driving car needs to have a virtual world model, which it then keeps updated with whatever it is receiving from the sensor fusion, which received its input from the sensor capture and the sensory devices.

D-04: System Action Plan

By having a virtual world model, the AI of the self-driving car is able to keep track of where the car is and what is happening around the car. In addition, the AI needs to determine what to do next. Should the self-driving car hit its brakes? Should the self-driving car stay in its lane or swerve into the lane to the left? Should the self-driving car accelerate or slow down?

A system action plan needs to be prepared by the AI of the self-driving car. The action plan specifies what actions should be taken. The actions need to pertain to the status of the virtual world model. Plus, the actions need to be realizable.

This realizability means that the AI cannot just assert that the self-driving car should suddenly sprout wings and fly. Instead, the AI must be bound by whatever the self-driving car can actually do, such as coming to a halt in a distance of X feet at a speed of Y miles per hour, rather than perhaps asserting that the self-driving car come to a halt in 0 feet as though it could instantaneously come to a stop while it is in motion.

D-05: Controls Activation

The system action plan is implemented by activating the controls of the car to act according to what the plan stipulates. This might mean that the accelerator control is commanded to increase the speed of the car. Or, the steering control is commanded to turn the steering wheel 30 degrees to the left or right.

One question arises as to whether or not the controls respond as they are commanded to do. In other words, suppose the AI has commanded the accelerator to increase, but for some reason it does not do so. Or, maybe it tries to do so, but the speed of the car does not increase. The controls activation feeds back into the virtual world model, and simultaneously the virtual world model is getting updated from the sensors, the sensor capture, and the sensor fusion. This allows the AI to ascertain what has taken place as a result of the controls being commanded to take some kind of action.

By the way, please keep in mind that though the diagram seems to have a linear progression to it, the reality is that these are all aspects of the self-driving car that are happening in parallel and simultaneously. The sensors are capturing data, meanwhile the sensor fusion is taking place, meanwhile the virtual model is being updated, meanwhile the system action plan is being formulated and reformulated, meanwhile the controls are being activated.

This is the same as a human being that is driving a car. They are eyeballing the road, meanwhile they are fusing in their mind the sights, sounds, etc., meanwhile their mind is updating their model of the world around them, meanwhile they are formulating an action plan of what to do, and meanwhile they are pushing their foot onto the pedals and steering the car. In the normal course of driving a car, you are doing all of these at once. I mention this so that when you look at the diagram, you will think of the boxes as processes that are all happening at the same time, and not as though only one happens and then the next.

They are shown diagrammatically in a simplistic manner to help comprehend what is taking place. You though should also realize that they are working in parallel and simultaneous with each other. This is a tough aspect in that the inter-element communications involve latency and other aspects that must be taken into account. There can be delays in one element updating and then sharing its latest status with other elements.

D-06: Automobile & CAN

Contemporary cars use various automotive electronics and a Controller Area Network (CAN) to serve as the components that underlie the driving aspects of a car. There are Electronic Control Units (ECU's) which control subsystems of the car, such as the engine, the brakes, the doors, the windows, and so on.

The elements D-01, D-02, D-03, D-04, D-05 are layered on top of the D-06, and must be aware of the nature of what the D-06 is able to do and not do.

D-07: In-Car Commands

Humans are going to be occupants in self-driving cars. In a Level 5 self-driving car, there must be some form of communication that takes place between the humans and the self-driving car. For example, I go into a self-driving car and tell it that I want to be driven over to Disneyland, and along the way I want to stop at In-and-Out Burger. The self-driving car now parses what I've said and tries to then establish a means to carry out my wishes.

In-car commands can happen at any time during a driving journey. Though my example was about an in-car command when I first got into my self-driving car, it could be that while the self-driving car is carrying out the journey that I change my mind. Perhaps after getting stuck in traffic, I tell the self-driving car to forget about getting the burgers and just head straight over to the theme park. The self-driving car needs to be alert to in-car commands throughout the journey.

D-08: V2X Communications

We will ultimately have self-driving cars communicating with each other, doing so via V2V (Vehicle-to-Vehicle) communications. We will also have self-driving cars that communicate with the roadways and other aspects of the transportation infrastructure, doing so via V2I (Vehicle-to-Infrastructure).

The variety of ways in which a self-driving car will be communicating with other cars and infrastructure is being called V2X, whereby the letter X means whatever else we identify as something that a car should or would want to communicate with. The V2X communications will be taking place simultaneous with everything else on the diagram, and those other elements will need to incorporate whatever it gleans from those V2X communications.

D-09: Deep Learning

The use of Deep Learning permeates all other aspects of the self-driving car. The AI of the self-driving car will be using deep learning to do a better job at the systems action plan, and at the controls activation, and at the sensor fusion, and so on.

Currently, the use of artificial neural networks is the most prevalent form of deep learning. Based on large swaths of data, the neural networks attempt to "learn" from the data and therefore direct the efforts of the self-driving car accordingly.

D-10: Tactical AI

Tactical AI is the element of dealing with the moment-to-moment driving of the self-driving car. Is the self-driving car staying in its lane of the freeway? Is the car responding appropriately to the controls commands? Are the sensory devices working?

For human drivers, the tactical equivalent can be seen when you watch a novice driver such as a teenager that is first driving. They are focused on the mechanics of the driving task, keeping their eye on the road while also trying to properly control the car.

D-11: Strategic AI

The Strategic AI aspects of a self-driving car are dealing with the larger picture of what the self-driving car is trying to do. If I had asked that the self-driving car take me to Disneyland, there is an overall journey map that needs to be kept and maintained.

There is an interaction between the Strategic AI and the Tactical AI. The Strategic AI is wanting to keep on the mission of the driving, while the Tactical AI is focused on the particulars underway in the driving effort. If the Tactical AI seems to wander away from the overarching mission, the Strategic AI wants to see why and get things back on track. If the Tactical AI realizes that there is something amiss on the self-driving car, it needs to alert the Strategic AI accordingly and have an adjustment to the overarching mission that is underway.

D-12: Self-Aware AI

Very few of the self-driving cars being developed are including a Self-Aware AI element, which we at the Cybernetic Self-Driving Car Institute believe is crucial to Level 5 self-driving cars.

The Self-Aware AI element is intended to watch over itself, in the sense that the AI is making sure that the AI is working as intended. Suppose you had a human driving a car, and they were starting to drive erratically. Hopefully, their own self-awareness would make them realize they themselves are driving poorly, such as perhaps starting to fall asleep after having been driving for hours on end. If you had a passenger in the car, they might be able to alert the driver if the driver is starting to do something amiss. This is exactly what the Self-Aware

AI element tries to do, it becomes the overseer of the AI, and tries to detect when the AI has become faulty or confused, and then find ways to overcome the issue.

D-13: Economic

The economic aspects of a self-driving car are not per se a technology aspect of a self-driving car, but the economics do indeed impact the nature of a self-driving car. For example, the cost of outfitting a self-driving car with every kind of possible sensory device is prohibitive, and so choices need to be made about which devices are used. And, for those sensory devices chosen, whether they would have a full set of features or a more limited set of features.

We are going to have self-driving cars that are at the low-end of a consumer cost point, and others at the high-end of a consumer cost point. You cannot expect that the self-driving car at the low-end is going to be as robust as the one at the high-end. I realize that many of the self-driving car pundits are acting as though all self-driving cars will be the same, but they won't be. Just like anything else, we are going to have self-driving cars that have a range of capabilities. Some will be better than others. Some will be safer than others. This is the way of the real-world, and so we need to be thinking about the economics aspects when considering the nature of self-driving cars.

D-14: Societal

This component encompasses the societal aspects of AI which also impacts the technology of self-driving cars. For example, the famous Trolley Problem involves what choices should a self-driving car make when faced with life-and-death matters. If the self-driving car is about to either hit a child standing in the roadway, or instead ram into a tree at the side of the road and possibly kill the humans in the self-driving car, which choice should be made?

We need to keep in mind the societal aspects will underlie the AI of the self-driving car. Whether we are aware of it explicitly or not, the AI will have embedded into it various societal assumptions.

D-15: Innovation

I included the notion of innovation into the framework because we can anticipate that whatever a self-driving car consists of, it will continue to be innovated over time. The self-driving cars coming out in the next several years will undoubtedly be different and less innovative than the versions that come out in ten years hence, and so on.

Framework Overall

For those of you that want to learn about self-driving cars, you can potentially pick a particular element and become specialized in that aspect. Some engineers are focusing on the sensory devices. Some engineers focus on the controls activation. And so on. There are specialties in each of the elements.

Researchers are likewise specializing in various aspects. For example, there are researchers that are using Deep Learning to see how best it can be used for sensor fusion. There are other researchers that are using Deep Learning to derive good System Action Plans. Some are studying how to develop AI for the Strategic aspects of the driving task, while others are focused on the Tactical aspects.

A well-prepared all-around software developer that is involved in self-driving cars should be familiar with all of the elements, at least to the degree that they know what each element does. This is important since whatever piece of the pie that the software developer works on, they need to be knowledgeable about what the other elements are doing.

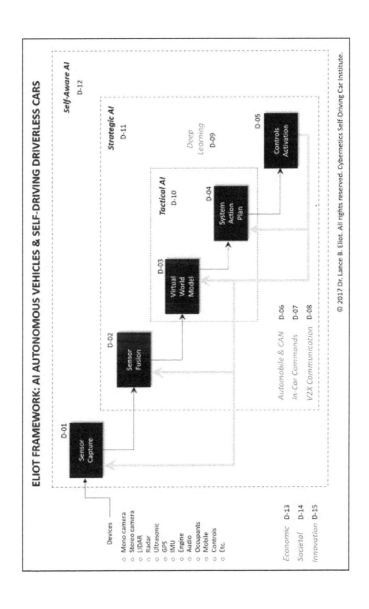

CHAPTER 2

OFF-ROADING
AND
AI SELF-DRIVING CARS

CHAPTER 2

OFF-ROADING
AND AI SELF-DRIVING CARS

Green laning. Mudding. Rock crawling. Dune bashing. These are all various kinds of off-road driving experiences. For those of you that happen to own or use an Off-Road Vehicle (ORV), I'm sure that you are smiling right now as I mention such as aspects a green laning, which involves driving an ORV on forest trails in a greenery environment, or perhaps you are more akin to doing dune bashing, which involves rolling up and down sand dunes at the beach.

Rock crawling can be particularly scary as you inch your ORV over the top of rocks and sometimes try to scale large-scale rock formations, doing so at steep and rather precarious angles. In contrast, mudding usually involves splashing and slipping and sliding your way through gooey mud. The mud wants to cling to every pore of the ORV and can even blind the driver by coating the windshield with a nearly impenetrably thick layer of mishmash dank mud.

Some people seem to select a particular kind of off-road environment and then stick with it, rather than aiming at all of the myriad of off-road possibilities.

There are the desert rats that always go to the open desert to do their off-roading. The mud slugs like those forest-like areas that have lots of rain and provide ample oodles of mud. Dune dogs are always found at the off-road opportunities on sandy beaches and you can just barely hear them over the roar of their engines as they yelp and holler upon bouncing over the next curvy dune.

Is off-roading a sport? There's a great deal of debate about whether driving your vehicle in these off-road situations is a sport or just some kind of hobby or pastime. For the true off-roaders, they would likely argue to the death that it is a sport. They often put their heart and soul into preparing their vehicles and love to compete against other off-roaders. You'll see them congregate at a muddy plot of land or at imposing rock formations and then see who can make it across or over these impediments, often clocking each other to see who can do so the fastest. There are points to be had for style. Plus, of course, not breaking your neck or your vehicle is considered notable too.

Not everyone is keen on having off-roaders do their thing. Various environmental entities have repeatedly sought to have off-roading corralled, doing so as a means to help protect public lands from potential harm or destruction. There are legal and illegal ways to do off-roading. At times, off-roading can harm animal habitats, it can destroy or hamper existing trails, it can degrade the land itself, it can produce pollution, and so on. Some say too that the noise produced is untoward and adversely impacts animals and even humans that otherwise might desire to enjoy the quiet outdoors. Numerous court cases have been brought by local agencies, state governments, the federal government, and have wound their way at times to the United States Supreme Court.

Do you have to use a specially equipped vehicle to do off-roading? No, you don't, and it all depends on what kind of off-road circumstance you are facing.

If you want to get or craft an ORV, there are lots of auto makers that provide consumer-oriented trucks, jeeps, and SUV's that are built for doing off-roading. You might need a reinforced roll cage to protect the occupants of the vehicle. You might need large super-thick tires with special traction. You might need high-clearance and underbody protection to keep from trashing the innards of your engine and transmission. Typically, you've got 4WD (four-wheel drive) and RWD (rear wheel drive), along with settings for different gears to be able to deal with the need for pushing power to your wheels. You've probably got tough shock absorbers with taut springs. Etc.

Some ORV's are classified as RTV's (Road Taxed Vehicles). An RTV is considered street-legal and able to drive on our everyday public roads, along with then shifting into an off-roading mode once the situation presents itself. Or, it could be that you opt to get an ORV that is not legally able to traverse on conventional roads, and if so you are likely to have a CCV (Cross Country Vehicle). The beauty for some off-roaders of having a CCV is that you can add or subtract automotive components and do so without having to be worried that you'll get a ticket for driving it on normal streets. These kinds of off-roaders will trick out their ORV with an anything-goes mindset.

What about using everyday conventional cars to do off-roading – can you do so? Yes, and I'd like to share some examples with you.

When I was earlier in my career doing consulting as a programmer-for-hire, I had gotten a call from a tech firm residing in Palo Alto, California that had gotten a contract to implement digital technology for a hotel casino in Las Vegas. Through the programmer avid grapevine, the tech firm had heard that I was a hotshot in the processors that they were going to use for automating the slot machines of the casino. After I briefly chatted with the director overseeing the project, he told me I was hired for the gig and that I should get ready to live in Vegas for the 5-weeks projects (they would be putting me up at the hotel casino for the duration of the effort).

Living in Southern California, I had been to Las Vegas numerous times before. Getting there is relatively easy. Besides the possibility of taking a 1-hour flight, most tend to just drive to Vegas since it is a somewhat quick drive of about 5 hours. On the drive there, you are dreaming about the riches you'll gain at the gambling tables and via the slot machines. On the drive back home, you are usually sulking at the money you lost, but at least you'll hopefully have fond memories of having had a good time.

The director in-charge of the project said that he'd drive down from Palo Alto to Los Angeles and pick me up on the way out to Las Vegas, and he'd be picking up another programmer that was in San Jose, doing so prior to reaching me in Southern California. The three of us would be able to get acquainted on the drive to Vegas and discuss the details of the effort. Seemed like an interesting project and one that would give me a chance to "live in Vegas" and see what that would be like (versus always having been a tourist). He told me that I would need to sign a nondisclosure agreement and that whatever happens in Vegas stays in Vegas.

Upon reaching me in Los Angeles, the three of us then got underway toward Vegas. Once you get outside of the major cities of the Los Angeles area, the rest of the journey to Vegas is through barren desert. There is a nice paved highway that stretches from the outskirts of Los Angeles and makes its way to Las Vegas, snaking its way across the vast landscape of the open desert. You can imagine that the Vegas operators want to make sure that those gamblers from Southern California that want to lose their money at the casinos have a handy means to get to Vegas. The highway seems to always be kept in rather pristine condition.

We were about an hour or so outside of Vegas when all of a sudden, the director asked if we wanted to see an old abandoned gold mine. Apparently, he had heard about a gold mine in the desert that used to have been very productive and ultimately was boarded up. He thought it would be neat to go see the closed-up mine. I wasn't keen on the idea. The other programmer was excited about the notion and urged that we take a look.

To my consternation, we slowed down upon coming to a dirt road that was an offshoot of the main highway while on our way to Vegas. We got off the main highway, a paved road that was clean and smooth, and instead began to drive on a rutted dirt road full of potholes and sagebrush. The director had rented a normal passenger car and it was not oriented at all toward doing any kind of off-road efforts. Nonetheless, there we were, bumping and wheeling along on a dirt road.

I looked out the back window of the car and gradually could see that the main highway was getting smaller and smaller as it disappeared from sight. The dirt road eventually weaved around various desert hills and we were then completely unseen from the main highway. Suppose the car broke down? I worried that no one taking the main highway to Vegas would be able to see us. If we wanted to walk to the main highway because of the car breaking down, it would likely take hours of marching through a hot desert. Once it got to nighttime, I knew too that the temperature would plunge to freezing conditions and the darkness in the desert can be dizzying (there weren't any street lights to be had).

Anyway, since the other two occupants were gleeful about seeing the gold mine, I opted to remain silent and just hoped for the best (side note: next time, if there ever is a next time, I'd insist to not take such a journey without proper preparation; nobody knew that we were taking this tangent and at least if we had told someone else it might have make things a bit more reasonable). After about 20 minutes of rumbling along the dirt road, we could see the boarded-up gold mine ahead.

Unfortunately, there wasn't even a road per se anymore and the car was now being driven on nothing more than uncultivated wild desert dirt. We slowed down to a crawling speed since the car was having a hard time dealing with the ruts and holes. It was like being inside a washing machine as the car whipped from side-to-side and we bumped along. This added about another 15 minutes of driving time, making our way only a seemingly short distance but was akin to being in the Mr. Toad's Wild Ride at Disneyland. If my teeth weren't going to be jarred out of my head, I certainly expected to have the car itself fall apart and leave strewn automobile parts like the bones and carcasses of deceased desert animals.

We pulled up to the opening of the gold mine. There was a large sign that proclaimed "Danger: Stay Out" and for which seemed to suggest to me that we ought to not go into the abandoned mine. Somehow, my two compatriots interpreted the sign as though it was beckoning us to come on in. They told me that of course there had to be a sign telling people not to go into the mine shaft, since whomever owned it had to try and avoid any liability. But they assured me, it was safe to go into this darkened, dirty, damp, forbidding mine and that everyone really "knew" that the sign was to be ignored.

I offered to stay outside of the mine. If they wanted to go into the mine, it was up to them. I would wait outside and be able to aid them or perhaps rescue them if needed. Admittedly, I wasn't sure what kind of a rescue I could do, other than going to get help. Keep in mind though that getting help was not going to be quick. It would require driving on the non-road to the dirt road, and then driving on the dirt road to the main highway, and then taking the main highway likely all the rest of the way to the outskirts of Vegas before I'd find even a gas station that could be sought for assistance.

My two colleagues were sure that I would be saddened to not go into the mine, and after realizing I was not going to set one foot into the open shaft (you could squeeze your way around the wood slats that had been placed across the opening to dissuade entry), they cheerfully started into the mine. I watched them until they gradually went out of view. I yelled to them a few times to check-in with them and eventually no longer got a reply. They had descended too far into the mine to hear me.

I stood next to the opening and looked at my watch. How long should I wait until they return? It was then that I realized something that I should not even admit to you. First, keep in mind that I was just in my early 20's and perhaps a bit naïve about the world. Okay, ready? I realized that the keys to the car were with the two colleagues that were now inside the mine and completely beyond reach. Yikes! Somehow in all of the excitement and debate about the mine, they had hung onto the keys and I had failed to get the keys from them. If help was needed, I would have to walk to the main highway and then try to plead with a passing car to stop and assist. The situation was a mess.

Whereas they had insisted they would just poke around in the mine and come right back out, it was nearly two hours later before they emerged from the mine. I suppose it was best that I didn't have the keys since I probably would have driven away to get help by the end of the first hour of their disappearance. Anyway, they relished bragging to me about the gold mine and after we drove back to the main highway and ultimately got to Vegas, they told everyone else on the team that it was the trip of a lifetime to have explored the abandoned mine. I still claim that they were lucky to have not gotten hurt, or gotten trapped, or who knows what could have happened.

The story provides an example of going off-road. Furthermore, we went off-road in a conventional car. I'd wager that people often use their conventional car for various off-road pursuits. Going off-road does not always need to be some massive off-road circumstance involving masses of mud and attempts at water fording. Instead, we face off-road situations all the time.

What does constitute going off-road?

For some people, if their GPS cannot map an area, they would say they are off-road. Have you ever driven to your local mall and gotten into the middle of the mall parking lot, and then asked your GPS to give you directions to get out of the mall? At times, the GPS won't have any map to refer to and will simply tell you to first find your own way to an identifiable road. The mall itself is considered "off-road" in that the GPS has no idea about the nature of the smaller streets and weaving paths within the confines of the mall.

There are various trail ratings that are used to gauge how difficult an off-road situation might be. This helps for those that are purposely going off-road to designated areas and they then can anticipate how easy or hard the off-road location might be. This also is handy for doing competitions because you can then say that you succeeded in a really easy off-road or a really hard off-road situation.

I'll offer this scale for purposes of trying to ascertain an off-road difficulty factor:

0: Not off-road
(an on-road situation and without any off-road aspects)

1: Borderline off-road
(mainly on-road with some easily navigated off-road)

2: Mild off-road
(off-road but likely ok for a conventional car)

3: Arduous off-road
(off-road and unlikely for a conventional car)

4: Grueling off-road
(requires an ORV and somewhat taxing)

5: Severe off-road
(ORV stretched to its limits)

6: Unnavigable off-road
(not navigable by a ground-based vehicle)

My side trip into the desert was a rating of 2. Trying to drive in a mall parking lot that has no GPS map is a 1.

You need to be thoughtful about the use of the scoring. For example, you might want to consider the worst-case portion of the off-road situation and rate the matter that way. If you are on a passable trail and reach a water fording that only a boat could handle, and suppose you need to turn back, the water hazard makes the overall path into a 5 or 6, even if the rest of the path was perhaps a 2 or 3.

There is another perspective too on the off-road situation. There are predicaments whereby the off-roading has come to you, rather than you going to it. Suppose you are at home and live in an area that is prone to hurricanes. You live in a quiet neighborhood with nice paved streets. Once a hurricane hits, it might rip up the roads, it might flood the roads, it might toss debris onto the roads. Thus, you went from normally driving entirely on-road to now having to drive "off-road" while still in your neighborhood.

Do not think of off-roading as only the use case involving going to some remote location and being prepared for becoming an off-roader. Off-roading can occur in our daily lives.

When I was in my teens, and just barely able to legally drive, I took a date to a movie theatre. It was our first date and I was hoping to impress. The movie theatre parking lot was full and as such the theatre had provided a dirt lot next door for overflow parking. I parked in the dirt lot and we proceeded into the theatre. Had a great time and watched a memorable movie.

Upon exiting the movie theatre, we discovered it had rained heavily while we were watching the movie. The dirt parking lot was now a sea of mud. I told my date to wait at the front of the movie theatre and I would go get the car out of the mud. When I tried to move the car, the tires just slid and could not get any traction. A couple of guys that were coming out to their cars offered to help push my car (I am still forever grateful!), and so I put the car in neutral and we all pushed to get the car onto dry land. As I stood along them at outside the car to help push it, I became utterly caked with mud. I then drove up to the front of the theatre and picked-up my date, feeling a bit foolish to have gotten stuck in the mud and now to be completely coated with mud. I guess that's Murphy's Law about first dates.

The point being that I was not in a remote locale. I had not driven up to the mountains or out into the desert. I was in the city and yet still had an off-road experience. You might want to argue about the nature of the off-road experience and say that it was pretty short-lived, Okay, sure, but I would argue that it nonetheless was an off-road activity.

What does this have to do with AI self-driving cars?

At the Cybernetic AI Self-Driving Car Institute, we are developing AI software for self-driving cars. One crucial aspect relates to off-roading. I'll explain more about the off-roading element in a moment.

I'd like to first clarify and introduce the notion that there are varying levels of AI self-driving cars. The topmost level is considered Level 5. A Level 5 self-driving car is one that is being driven by the AI and there is no human driver involved. For the design of Level 5 self-driving cars, the auto makers are even removing the gas pedal, brake pedal, and steering wheel, since those are contraptions used by human drivers. The Level 5 self-driving car is not being driven by a human and nor is there an expectation that a human driver will be present in the self-driving car. It's all on the shoulders of the AI to drive the car.

For self-driving cars less than a Level 5, there must be a human driver present in the car. The human driver is currently considered the responsible party for the acts of the car. The AI and the human driver are co-sharing the driving task. In spite of this co-sharing, the human is supposed to remain fully immersed into the driving task and be ready at all times to perform the driving task. I've repeatedly warned about the dangers of this co-sharing arrangement and predicted it will produce many untoward results.

Let's focus herein on the true Level 5 self-driving car. Much of the comments apply to the less than Level 5 self-driving cars too, but the fully autonomous AI self-driving car will receive the most attention in this discussion.

Here's the usual steps involved in the AI driving task:
- Sensor data collection and interpretation
- Sensor fusion
- Virtual world model updating
- AI action planning
- Car controls command issuance

Another key aspect of AI self-driving cars is that they will be driving on our roadways in the midst of human driven cars too. There are some pundits of AI self-driving cars that continually refer to a Utopian world in which there are only AI self-driving cars on the public roads. Currently there are about 250+ million conventional cars in the United States alone, and those cars are not going to magically disappear or become true Level 5 AI self-driving cars overnight.

Indeed, the use of human driven cars will last for many years, likely many decades, and the advent of AI self-driving cars will occur while there are still human driven cars on the roads. This is a crucial point since this means that the AI of self-driving cars needs to be able to contend with not just other AI self-driving cars, but also contend with human driven cars. It is easy to envision a simplistic and rather unrealistic world in which all AI self-driving cars are politely interacting with each other and being civil about roadway interactions. That's not what is going to be happening for the foreseeable future. AI self-driving cars and human driven cars will need to be able to cope with each other.

Returning to the topic of off-roading, here's something that might knock your socks off. According to the official Levels of self-driving cars, a Level 5 self-driving car does not necessarily need to be able to handle off-road driving.

As per the SAE standard, a Level 5 self-driving car is supposed to be able to drive the car for all driver-manageable on-road conditions. Notice that there are then two important caveats. One caveat is that the driving circumstances must be driver-manageable. The other caveat is that the driving situations apply only to on-road and not off-road occasions.

We can argue about what is a driver-manageable circumstance, and likewise we can argue about what is off-road versus on-road. Let's consider separately at first the driver-manageable aspects. We'll then consider the off-road versus on-road aspects. And, I'll then intertwine the two elements since they can indeed intersect with each other.

A driver-manageable situation involves a driving task that presumably a human could drive. If a human could not drive the car, it might be "unfair" to expect that the AI can somehow magically drive the car. For example, my car is pinned in, sandwiched among other cars in a parking lot. As a human, no matter what I do, I cannot drive my car out of the situation. I'm stuck. We could not reasonably expect that the AI can drive the car out of the situation either. It is not a driver-manageable circumstance, whether by human or by automation.

The grey area of being driver-manageable though involves the nature of the driver. I was stuck in the snow one time and thought I could not drive my way out. A highway patrol officer stopped to take a look at my stuck car. He offered to help and then actually got into my car and drove it out of the snow. If you had asked me beforehand if it was a driver-manageable circumstance, I might have said that it was not. I might have insisted that there was no means to drive the car out of the snow. You can see that this example illustrates the potential for a grey area of what is driver-manageable or not. It can at times be in the eye of the beholder and in the skillset of the driver.

Next, let's consider the notion of Level 5 not being required to deal with off-road situations. What is an on-road versus an off-road circumstance?

I don't think you can say that off-road is only when you are driving an ORV. As my earlier examples illustrate, you can get yourself into an off-road driving situation and not be in a vehicle that was intended for off-roading per se. A conventional car can just as readily be involved in off-roading. Therefore, you cannot dictate that the type of car ergo means you are off-roading (plus, of course, you might be using an ORV while driving on normal highways, therefore you are using it for both on-road driving and off-road driving).

You cannot claim that off-roading is solely when you are in a remote location. My story about the movie theatre parking lot shows that you can be immersed in a city environment and still do off-road driving. Likewise, as mentioned, off-roading can come to you, such as my example of the hurricane that strikes your neighborhood.

For some pundits, off-roading involves going outside the bounds of your GPS.

To them, when being even in a mall parking lot, and if your GPS cannot provide a map of your location, it is off-roading because the GPS can no longer provide navigation instructions about the car for you.

This is partially why there is a huge effort afoot to try and digitally map every square inch of populated areas. For an AI self-driving car, if it has no map to showcase where to go, in some respects that AI becomes unable to navigate the car. Sure, the AI can still drive the car, but where is it intended to drive to? There is a kind of push toward the Holy Grail of having detailed maps of everywhere that you might want to go, which then will make life easier for the AI of the self-driving car.

Having AI system such as robots navigate an unmapped area and gradually figure out as much as it can about the area is a well-known and much studied problem in computer science, and it is more commonly referred to as SLAM, which is an acronym for Simultaneous Localization And Mapping. We will gradually see this same kind of technique used by AI self-driving cars that find themselves in unmapped areas.

I think you can guess why the Level 5 includes the carve-out that the topmost level only involves on-road situations. For on-road driving, presumably you would have a map that informs the AI about where you are driving and it would be coupled to a GPS. For off-road driving, there is less likely to be any map available of where to go. It is a harder driving situation.

Also, off-roading tends to involve tricky driving. Driving in thick mud is trickier than driving on a dry paved road. Driving in the snow is trickier than driving on a rain covered road. Driving over dunes at the beach can be quite tricky, especially if you are not wanting to roll the vehicle over. Etc.

When I refer to driving as being tricky, this dovetails us into the other aspect of the Level 5 about being driver-manageable. Someone that drives their car each day to work on paved roads might be quite taken aback if you asked them to try and drive across rocks and boulders in the desert. There is a skill involved in handling off-road driving.

We are faced then with situations that are off-road and challenging, and also circumstances where there is a question if the driving is driver-manageable or not. Often, an off-road situation is also one that tends to be driver-manageable challenging. Obviously, you can have on-road situations that are also driver-manageable challenging, but I'd say it is fair to suggest that more-often-than-not an off-road situation will likely be also driver-manageable challenging, more so than an on-road driving task.

I have had AI developers that tell me they are relieved that the Level 5 does not require an AI skillset that involves doing off-roading. These AI developers are swamped with trying to get self-driving cars to merely navigate on-road and make sure that the AI doesn't injure or kill anyone as it does so. It is nearly unimaginable to those AI developers that they might have to also deal with the vagaries of off-roading.

I am doubtful though that consumers are going to be happy to discover that their vaunted AI self-driving car does not necessarily know how to cope with off-road driving situations. It might be reasonable as an auto maker to say that your AI self-driving car cannot handle driving in some obscure unexplored outback location, but if it won't get you out of a muddy parking lot at a movie theatre, I'd bet that people will howl about such a limitation.

Similarly, suppose you have your AI self-driving car parked at home, and a hurricane causes wanton destruction and damage to the streets of your neighborhood. If the AI of the self-driving car considers such a road to now be off-road, you are going to be stuck. Furthermore, since there might not be any driving controls provided in the Level 5 self-driving car, you cannot drive yourself out of the situation, though you might want to do so.

Another somewhat disturbing concern too about the levels of self-driving cars is that a carve-out for off-road situations even exists without some other level to include it. What are we to call an AI self-driving car that can-do off-road driving? You could say it is Level 5, but now we'll have some Level 5 self-driving cars that can handle off-road driving and others that cannot. It would seem prudent to include another level, perhaps Level 6, which would include off-road driving.

I'm sure that someone will right away balk at having a Level 6 that includes off-road driving because they would argue that you cannot guarantee that an AI self-driving car could cope with all the possibilities of off-road driving. I hear you on that objection. But, let's make sure to remember that we can limit things by saying that it needs to be driver manageable. In essence, we could suggest that a Level 6 would include off-road but only when driver-manageable. I realize this provides a kind of loophole as to what off-road situations apply, but I think it reasonable to do so.

As an aside, if you want to know about another argument on this topic of driver-manageable, I've so far suggested that the definition of driver-manageable encompasses only if a human could have driven the car in the matter at-hand. I also raised the point that human drivers vary in their driving skills, such as me versus the highway patrol officer that was able to get me out of a snow jam. Let's pretend we decide that driver-manageable includes driving to the capability of the greatest possible driving that any human could drive. This then deals with the potential for having sub-par drivers, such as me and snow driving.

There are some pundits that suggest that the AI might be able to driver better than even the best of any human driver. Therefore, if we limit the definition of driver-manageable to only what the best human can drive, we are not allowing for the possibility that an AI driving system might eclipse human driving capabilities. As such, in theory, we need to posit that the driver-manageable definition encompasses not only the best human driver, but also includes whatever an AI driving system might be able to achieve that presumably could surpass the capabilities of humans.

Anyway, for now, the Level 5 indicates that the AI only needs to be able to deal with on-road situations. It is going to be ambiguous as to what constitutes on-road versus off-road. The auto makers and tech firms will likely be shaping these boundaries as they go along. You'll see a Level 5 self-driving car that strictly sticks with no off-road of any kind. Another auto maker or tech firm might try to best that by having a Level 5 self-driving car that can handle the borderline and mild forms of off-road. Competition will undoubtedly gradually get us toward AI self-driving cars that can handle various kinds of off-road situations.

There will also likely be AI systems developed for ORV's. You might assume that if there is AI that can cope with an ORV, it would seem a simple matter to then download the AI into a non-off-road self-driving car and it could too handle going off-road. The problem there is that the ORV is bound to be designed and built for off-road purposes. It might have the high-clearance, the special tires, and other equipment that allows it to handle off-road situations that a normal non-off-road self-driving car could not.

This also brings up the aspects of the sensors on a self-driving car. Today's sensors that are being used on self-driving cars are quite limited in their capacity to detect the kinds of objects and ground surface novelties that you would find when going truly off-roading. We are likely to see advances in sensor technology that will make sensors more capable for that kind of detection. Will we see those advanced sensors be included in everyday self-driving cars? Maybe yes, maybe not. The cost might be high so instead those sensors might get included into a pricier ORV.

Recall that I earlier mentioned that environmentalists and others are concerned that off-roading can damage or destroy land and wildlife, and can be disturbing to those that are not off-roading and trying to otherwise enjoy remote locales.

One question to consider is whether or not the AI self-driving car might be electronically prohibited from going into certain off-road locations.

You might have a human that wants to go into an off-road location for the spirit of doing so, but it could be an area deemed as not legally allowed for off-roading. In that case, it would be conceivable that the AI might have been notified that it is not to drive the car in such a locale. Today, if a human decides to sneakily drive in a closed-off or banned off-road area, they can pretty much try to do so and maybe not get caught. In the case of an AI self-driving car, presumably the AI itself might be notified that it is not to take the vehicle into such areas.

We'll need to see how the ethics of this plays out, and whether there are regulatory restrictions that might arise.

Here's another twist for you. Suppose the AI proceeds to go off-road, presumably at the request of the human occupants. While driving up one of those really steep rock climbs, the AI cannot handle it properly and the self-driving car tumbles off the rock. The human occupants are injured or killed. Would the auto maker and tech firm that made the AI be liable? You could say that it depends upon what claimed capability the AI self-driving car had for being able to go off-road. I'm sure clever lawyers would assert that the AI should have never gotten the self-driving car into an off-road situation for which the potential for harm was feasible.

Speaking of human occupants, there's another angle to this off-roading topic that is worthy of attention, namely the role of human passengers when an AI self-driving car is off-roading.

If there are human occupants inside an AI self-driving car when it goes off-roading, should the AI be conversing with those human occupants? For example, the AI self-driving car comes up to a water fording predicament. The AI is unsure whether the vehicle can make it across the water. Maybe it can, maybe it cannot. There is uncertainty involved.

The AI might ask the human occupants whether they are willing to have the AI take the risk of trying the water fording. If you are inside the self-driving car and trying to flee from a hurricane, you probably are willing to take the risk. If you are merely making your way to the candy store, you'd perhaps tell the AI that you don't want it to try and cross the water.

This raises all sorts of complications. Imagine that the only occupants are small children. They were put into the AI self-driving car by their parents and sent along, while the parents had perhaps no idea beforehand that a situation might arise involving the water fording possibility. Now, the AI is asking those young children to make a potential life-or-death decision. If you argue that the AI should ask the parents, you are making an assumption that the parents are reachable electronically, which I would dare say might not be feasible and especially if the self-driving car is in an off-road situation.

Another variant involves having an AI self-driving car that has no human occupants in it, meaning that at the time of going off-road, there is a chance that the self-driving car is merely trying to get to point B from some earlier point A. Or, it might have been commanded by a human that told the AI self-driving car to go ahead and do the dune bashing. Should an AI self-driving car be able to drive in off-road situations and not have any human occupants?

I suppose it could be that I was at the old gold mine and opted to go into it with my two colleagues and we all three got trapped. If we had an AI self-driving car that had brought us to the mine, it could be that it was timing our exit and if we did not appear after two hours, it would proceed to go get help. Kind of a modern-day version of Lassie. I think we can easily make the case that we would indeed expect an AI self-driving car to be able to deal with off-road situations regardless of whether humans are present in the AI self-driving car or not.

One means to potentially aid an AI self-driving car when it has opted to go off-road would be the use of V2V (vehicle-to-vehicle) electronic communications.

For the gold mine story, if I had gotten stuck with my colleagues in the gold mine, the AI self-driving car might have just stayed in front of the mine and merely used V2V to alert cars passing along on the main highway that we were in trouble.

The V2V could also be used among several AI self-driving cars to work together when dealing with an off-road driving situation. One AI self-driving car that has come upon a nearly impassable water fording might caution other following AI self-driving cars to turnaround and find a different way to go. Tips and suggestions about the off-road areas could be shared. This would especially be helpful if you assume that the area has no or poor GPS and no maps. The collective AI self-driving cars might be able to map things out, each offering a portion of the bigger picture.

Another means to gradually figure out off-road situations would involve the use of Machine Learning (ML), and particularly deep learning and the use of artificial neural networks.

When multiple AI self-driving cars have gone to a particular off-road location, the data collected by the sensors could be fed into the cloud of the auto maker or tech firm via OTA (Over-The-Air) electronic communications.

This data could be combined together and assessed by the ML. Patterns of the locale could be identified. Essentially, a map could be derived and the ways in which to navigate the area could possibly be pattern matched.

The results of the deep learning could then be fed back down into the AI self-driving cars of the fleet. This would allow other AI self-driving cars that had not yet experienced the particulars of the off-road locale to then potentially be able to do so.

Indeed, the overall capability of handling off-road situations should also hopefully be increased. Thus, it would be the case that the ML not only learns from a specific off-road situation, but also generalizes so that other off-road situations of a similar nature could also be better dealt with.

Some might argue that going truly off-roading is something that humans would want to do as human drivers.

In other words, even if the AI can handle going off-road, the excitement of going off-roading can only be gleaned if you are sitting in the driver's seat.

As such, there might still be cars that allow for humans to takeover the controls, doing so in limited situations such as off-road competitions and the like. Others might insist that no humans should be able to drive a Level 5 self-driving car, regardless of the reason.

Can you get as much joy from being a passenger as you can being a driver? Suppose the AI allows you to direct it while you are off-roading – would that be sufficient as a kind of "back-seat" driver rather than being directly at the driving controls? Time will tell.

I'm reminded of the famous line by off-road driver Ivan Stewart that there needs to be a sense of style in how you off-road and he coined the phrase CAR (Comfortable, Accurate, Relaxed).

He had said that if you have a cup of coffee in a cup holder and it is spilling over or in danger of falling out, you are not doing off-road driving to its pinnacle.

Merely navigating a muddy road or climbing a rock is not sufficient, you also need to do it with style and grace. This presumably also coincides with providing safety to the off-road experience and helping to ensure that humans are not harmed.

I suppose we need to first get the AI to be able to cope with off-roading, and once we've gotten that far, we can then aim for the stylishness elements.

I assure you though that we are going to need AI that can cope with going off-road. It might be the little kinds of off-roads of life like my movie theatre muddy parking lot, or it might be seeking gold at an abandoned mine in the middle of a desert. Off-road, it's a thing to be dealt with.

Let's step-up to the challenge.

CHAPTER 3

PARALLELING VEHICLES
AND
AI SELF-DRIVING CARS

CHAPTER 3

PARALLELING VEHICLES AND AI SELF-DRIVING CARS

I was on a mountainous highway that large trucks use to haul goods from Los Angeles up to San Francisco. There were two lanes going northbound. The inner lane hugged the mountain and was considered the slow lane. The lane to the left of the slow lane was considered the fast lane and it was perched at the edge of cliffs, from which if you drove a few feet to your left you'd plummet hundreds of feet to surely your death at the bottom of the canyons.

I'd driven this path many times and was used to the notion that there would be a slew of trucks in the slow lane as they lumbered up the mountains. It was tough for the trucks to make the climb and you could see that the drivers had the trucks in their lowest gears. Trucks that were full of merchandise or fruit or perhaps mailed packages were going exceedingly slow. As such, trucks that had no load or were loaded lightly had a tendency to try and pass the slower trucks by swinging over into the fast lane. Unfortunately, swinging into the fast lane for a rather slow truck was not conducive to car traffic that was using the fast lane to speed through the mountain pass.

On this particular day, there was almost no car traffic and it was just me and lots of unwieldy trucks. I kept my eyes open to spot any truck that might try to suddenly move into my fast lane, otherwise I seemed to be unimpeded and was able to push along at the maximum speed limit. It was somewhat eerie that I was moving past these trucks as though I was the hare and they were the turtles. Truck after truck likely saw me pass them as though I was moving at the speed of light. I don't know if those drivers ever get speed envy while making the run through the mountains, but at least I hoped they would be paying attention to faster moving cars and not make any sudden moves into the fast lane.

Some people don't put much thought into the act of passing a truck. They just seem to lollygag and are oblivious to the fact that while passing a truck they are at a distinct disadvantage on the roadway. Let's consider some of the dangers involved.

The moment that your car begins to pass a truck, you are now adjacent to a large and "immovable" object. You then are continuously at risk as you proceed alongside the truck. In my case, while being in the leftmost lane, it meant that I had a truck to my right that blocked any possibility of my being able to go to my right as an evasive driving tactic. Suppose that there was debris in the fast lane and I didn't spot it until the last moment, in which case, I really could not try to escape to my right due to the bulky truck in the road and would instead have to strike the debris head-on (assuming that I was unable to stop in time).

For the entire time from the start of passing the truck to the popping out ahead of the truck, it as though you are now without a parachute. The entire right side was no longer an open path for me to use and I might as well have been driving next to a brick wall. I realize you could suggest that if needed too I might try to ram the truck by shoving against the side of it with my car, but I assure you that by-and-large that approach is not going to gain you much. Yes, the truck might move over by the physics of hitting it, or the driver of the truck might realize that you are ramming the truck and the driver might then try to move over, though all-in-all it's not much of a saving grace and you'd be better served to pretend it is a relatively immovable wall.

My escape possibilities on this rather narrow two-lane mountain highway were slim. I could not swerve to the left because I'd go flying off a cliff. The trucks in the slow lane could not swerve to their right because the mountain was there to stop them from doing so.

Whenever I put a truck between me and the mountain, it was as though I was now in a one lane road and my only recourse was to deal with whatever might happen in my one lane. It was like a tunnel that once you entered into one end, you pretty much were stuck until you popped out the other end. The truck was one side of the tunnel and the edge of the cliff was the other side of the tunnel.

My strategy for dealing with passing the trucks was to make sure that I had good speed as I came up to the edge of a truck that was in the right lane. I do this because I want to be able to speed along past the truck. Some car drivers don't think about this aspect and are just cruising along at the prevailing speed. Once they get alongside a truck, sometimes the car driver awakens to the risks and tries to speed-up at that point. In my view, you are better off making a run up to it and try to rocket past the truck.

The basis for wanting to speed past the truck is to minimize the amount of time that you are locked into the "tunnel" that I've described earlier. Since there is such heightened risk while inside the virtual tunnel, you ought to try and minimize the amount of time that you are stuck in there. The longer your passing time, the longer your risk exists. Also, the more time that passes there is a likely greater chance of something going amiss. By trying to keep the passing time as low as feasible, you are hopefully reducing the odds that if something untoward is going to happen that it will happen while you are inside the virtual tunnel.

So, speeding past the truck will reduce the length of time and the distance involved in the passing operation. You also need to try and look ahead and anticipate your next move. It is like a game of chess. In chess play, you are looking at your next immediate move, and also trying to look ahead and the next moves. Each move ahead is considered a ply. A good chess player tries to consider several ply ahead and consider the moves and counter-moves that might occur. You should not make your immediate move until you've well-considered the subsequent moves.

In the case of passing a truck, you need to consider where the truck is, where you are, and what might occur during the time and distance of the passing operation. Suppose the truck is coming up to the bumper of a slower moving truck. If you try to pass the truck to its left, the truck driver is now stuck behind a slower moving truck and your car that is pinning the truck into the rightmost lane. The truck driver is not going to like this predicament. You have forced the truck into a tunnel of its own, along with now a truck ahead of the truck that is blocking the tunnel for that exasperated truck driver.

I mention the exasperated truck driver because there are times that I've seen cars start toward the edge of a truck as though the car wants to pass, but the truck driver realizes that allowing the car to pass will pin the truck behind say a slower moving truck. As such, the truck driver, playing a bit of mental chess of driving, might opt to swing over into the fast lane, doing so to block the car driver from cutting off the truck from that possibility. Plus, the truck driver was likely going to soon swing into the fast lane to pass the lumbering truck. What happened is that the truck driver initiated their move into the fast lane prematurely due to seeing that a car was going to time things to cut them off when they really wanted to pass.

A good car driver would have anticipated this kind of action by the truck driver. The car driver should have not only been paying attention to their own lane. A savvy car driver needs to consider all lanes of traffic and all nearby vehicles of traffic. What is in the mind of the truck driver whose truck you are about to pass? Will that truck driver let you pass, or will they try to cut you off before you can pass?

Even more worrisome is the possibility that the truck driver might lose sight of your car and thus cut you off once you are already committed to making the passing move. I'm sure you've seen situations wherein a sneaky car tries to snake past the side of a truck and the truck driver inadvertently either bashes the car or appears likely to do so because the truck starts to move into the lane. It could be the truck driver was somewhat asleep at the wheel and wasn't paying attention to the traffic. Or, it could be that the car ended-up in the blind spot of the truck and the truck driver lost sight of the car. Or, it could be that the car was sly and essentially fooled the driver into not realizing the car was there. It could also be a joint confusion of both the car driver and the truck driver, each not practicing appropriately safe driving tactics.

For each of the trucks that I opted to pass while on the mountain road, in each case I carefully scrutinized the traffic situation. Was there any truck in front of the truck that I was about to pass, and if so, how far away was the lead truck? Would I be able to quickly make it past the truck that I wanted to pass, or was there anything ahead of me in my lane that might forestall such an attempt? Could I get up to my desired passing speed or was there some reason that I would not be able to do so? Once I got alongside the truck, did there appear to be anything arising that might make the risks even worse of being inside the virtual tunnel that I was about to create?

Keep in mind that I passed probably fifty or so trucks during that hour of driving through the mountain passes. This means that I had to calculate the contortions of the passing effort about every minute of driving time. Some drivers would get weary of the matter and probably just decide to wing it upon each attempt at passing a truck. It might be like being a batter at a baseball game whereby they kept pitching you ball after ball. The first few baseballs you might carefully hunch over and be grabbing your bat, and then gradually you lose your edge and just keep swinging at whatever comes across the plate. Of course, the act of passing trucks is a life-or-death matter and not the same as simply trying to hit a baseball out of the park.

As luck would have it, and given the volume of pass attempts, I had one instance that got my heart pounding and my hands gripped the wheel in a steely manner. You could say it was partially due to an error on my part of my mental calculations about passing.

I was coming up to a truck that was in the right lane, the slow lane. There was a truck ahead of him but at a far enough distance that this truck driver would not likely be thinking yet about switching lanes. My lane ahead was unimpeded. There were no cars or trucks directly behind me. I had the runway needed to get up to my desired passing speed. It all seemed a go.

I got up to my passing speed and timed it so that I was then at the rear edge of the truck. I would hopefully fly past the truck and soon pop out ahead of the truck. The truck though suddenly and unexpectedly slightly edged into my lane. The truck driver did not seem to be trying to move into my lane. Nor did the truck driver seem to be trying to send me a subtle signal to stay out of the lane by edging into it (which, sometimes they might do intentionally or unintentionally).

We were on a part of the mountain road that was somewhat curvy. This brings up another factor about the act of passing trucks. Trying to pass a truck on a blind curve is fraught with greater risks. The truck driver might not tightly take the curve and thus use part of your lane for making the curve. The truck driver might not even realize that perhaps the back portion of their truck is not able to make the curve fully within their own lane and the rear-end slides over nudgingly into your lane. You also likely cannot readily gauge what is in the road ahead due to the curvature of the road. Etc.

In this instance, we weren't at an actual curve per se, which if we had been at a true curve, I would have been much less likely to try and make the passing move. Nonetheless, the road was somewhat curvy. I'd guess that the truck driver somehow lost awareness about the lane and the slight curvature aspects.

Fortunately, I had not made a firm commitment to the passing act and could back-down since I was only still at the rear-edge of the truck. I had to tap my brakes to trim down my speed and allow the truck at its speed to continue forward, thus, I essentially receded from the passing act and the truck pulled ahead of my passing act.

This moment of fright was just a few split seconds. Yet, I remember it vividly. That's the way driving often comes out to be. You might have lots of time of nothing eventual, and then you suddenly have a short happening that takes just a split second and it could be something you'll remember the rest of your life. In this case, the incident was so minimal that I would not even say it registers as being memorable – no one hit anyone, no one else was in the car with me that might have also been shocked, and so on. I've had other such incidents that were much worse, and I'm sure you've had many of your own too.

What does this have to do with AI self-driving cars?

At the Cybernetic AI Self-Driving Car Institute, we are developing AI software for self-driving cars. One crucial driving tactic for the AI involves awareness of paralleling vehicles and what to do about it.

Allow me to elaborate.

I'd like to first clarify and introduce the notion that there are varying levels of AI self-driving cars. The topmost level is considered Level 5. A Level 5 self-driving car is one that is being driven by the AI and there is no human driver involved. For the design of Level 5 self-driving cars, the auto makers are even removing the gas pedal, brake pedal, and steering wheel, since those are contraptions used by human drivers. The Level 5 self-driving car is not being driven by a human and nor is there an expectation that a human driver will be present in the self-driving car. It's all on the shoulders of the AI to drive the car.

For self-driving cars less than a Level 5, there must be a human driver present in the car. The human driver is currently considered the responsible party for the acts of the car. The AI and the human driver are co-sharing the driving task. In spite of this co-sharing, the human is supposed to remain fully immersed into the driving task and be ready at all times to perform the driving task. I've repeatedly warned about the dangers of this co-sharing arrangement and predicted it will produce many untoward results.

Let's focus herein on the true Level 5 self-driving car. Much of the comments apply to the less than Level 5 self-driving cars too, but the fully autonomous AI self-driving car will receive the most attention in this discussion.

Here's the usual steps involved in the AI driving task:
- Sensor data collection and interpretation
- Sensor fusion
- Virtual world model updating
- AI action planning
- Car controls command issuance

Another key aspect of AI self-driving cars is that they will be driving on our roadways in the midst of human driven cars too. There are some pundits of AI self-driving cars that continually refer to a utopian world in which there are only AI self-driving cars on the public roads. Currently there are about 250+ million conventional cars in the United States alone, and those cars are not going to magically disappear or become true Level 5 AI self-driving cars overnight.

Indeed, the use of human driven cars will last for many years, likely many decades, and the advent of AI self-driving cars will occur while there are still human driven cars on the roads. This is a crucial point since this means that the AI of self-driving cars needs to be able to contend with not just other AI self-driving cars, but also contend with human driven cars. It is easy to envision a simplistic and rather unrealistic world in which all AI self-driving cars are politely interacting with each other and being civil about roadway interactions. That's not what is going to be happening for the foreseeable future. AI self-driving cars and human driven cars will need to be able to cope with each other.

Returning to the topic of paralleling vehicles, I know that some AI pundits would argue that there is no real need to be especially mindful about the topic because AI self-driving cars will presumably all have V2V (vehicle-to-vehicle) electronic communications. As such, the moment that a self-driving car tries to pass another vehicle, all the AI needs to do is let the other vehicle know that passing is about to happen. The other vehicle, having gotten the electronic communication, will presumably politely acknowledge the passing action and help ensure that it happens unimpeded.

This might work in a world filled of AI self-driving vehicles, but as mentioned earlier this is not going to happen to our world for many decades to come. I certainly agree that the use of V2V will be very handy and that for those AI self-driving cars and trucks that are equipped with V2V it will be boon to safety. Meanwhile, the real-world is that there will be human car drivers and there will be human truck drivers, and the ability to undertake V2V with those human driven vehicles will be less likely. Cross out for now the "solution" of paralleling is simply to invoke V2V.

Okay, I trust that you are therefore still with me on the notion that the AI will need to have a means to deal with the paralleling aspects. I'd wager that most of you are agreeable that the AI should have a special capability that deals with paralleling other vehicles.

You might be surprised to know that not everyone sees this as a "problem" in its own right. There are some AI developers that suggest the paralleling matter is a non-matter. Let's consider my story about passing various trucks on the mountain road. The simpleton approach would be that if the fast lane is available then it makes no difference whether I am passing a truck or not passing truck. All the AI needs to do is keep focused on driving in the fast lane. Until or if the self-driving car wants to switch into the slow lane, there is presumably no need to even be aware of the trucks that are lumbering in the slow lane.

This is the classic pied piper approach to AI driving. The AI merely follows a vehicle ahead of it, and if there isn't a vehicle directly ahead then just proceed at the speed limit or a speed allowed as per the nature of the road conditions. No need to be watching other lanes. All the AI needs to do is detect whether there is anything in its prevailing lane. No blockages, no debris, no trucks, and so the AI assumes all is glorious and the self-driving car can merely drive along.

This is the lollygag kind of human driving that I referred to earlier. Not a care in the world. You can put on blinders and just ignore everything but the lane and what's in it. If a truck is going to switch lanes, well, you'll see it when it happens. Plus, logically, it makes no sense that a truck would attempt to switch lanes while you are occupying the lane as you are passing the truck, and since it is not a logical move by the truck then there is no reason to consider it as a possibility.

Admittedly, this novice teenager driving style might work much of the time. You might be lucky and go for quite a while without having any incidents. Congrats. But I would wager that ultimately this blind and narrow kind of driving will catch-up with you. All it will take is that truck driver that catches you completely off-guard and you'll end-up in a tough predicament. Furthermore, you'll be utterly ill-prepared to take any evasive action. I certainly don't think we want our AI systems for self-driving cars to be driving in a lollygag manner.

Overall, I'd assert that the AI needs to be capable of dealing with the paralleling aspects. Notice that I am not merely labeling this as the passing of vehicles, and instead referring to this act as the notion of paralleling. Let me explain why.

As a car driver, I'm sure you find yourself frequently being parallel to other vehicles. This is common. It happens not merely when you are overtly trying to pass another vehicle. You might be on the freeway and traffic is clogged. You have cars to your left and to your right. You are not necessarily trying to go past them. You are merely moving back-and-forth in your lane, and they are moving back-and-forth in their lanes, and you are all crawling along on the snarled freeway.

I think it is vital that any driver, whether human or AI, be aware of the act of paralleling. The moment you are parallel to another vehicle, you are now within inches of the other vehicle. This means that the chances of getting into an incident with those other vehicles is increased. There is less wiggle room, as it were. This is true of having trucks next to you and equally true when having cars next to you.

The nice thing about having a car parallel to you is that the length of the car is likely a lot less than the length of a truck. Because of the shorter length of the car, there is less time you are likely paralleling the car and also less distance when paralleling. I state this with a grain of salt because you need to realize that you can be paralleling any vehicle for lengthy time periods. If I am on the freeway and jammed in traffic,

I might be next to a truck for many minutes at a time, and likewise next to a car for many minutes at a time.

Here's something that happens to me from time-to-time and I'd guess happens to you too. I am on the freeway and cruising along. The freeway is wide open. A car comes in the lane next to me and is going at a faster speed. I am anticipating that car will become parallel to me in a few moments and will continue ahead at their existing pace, thus, the car will only be parallel to me for a split second or two. It will be a momentary and transitory act.

Instead, the car comes up and then opts to unexpectedly slow down and goes perfectly parallel to my car. It's kind of bizarre when it happens. Note that there is nothing ahead of the car and so it is unimpeded. Also, had the car kept going at its prevailing speed, it would have clearly passed me already and gone ahead of me. Nor did I change my speed such that I was now somehow going at a faster speed that would have forced me into become parallel with the other car once it caught up with me. I'm claiming that there is absolutely no apparent driving reason for this other car to have decided to slow down and run parallel to my car.

Have you had this happen to you?

One possible explanation on open highways could be that the other driver believes they might stick out like a sore thumb if they are exceeding the speed limit. By paralleling my car, perhaps the other driver thinks that a cop won't ticket them, or that if a cop is going to do something there are now two choices rather than one.

Another possible explanation is that the driver was not really aware of how fast they were going. They arrived at my car and decided that they were going too fast. They decide therefore to slow down. This puts them parallel to my car on an enduring basis. The other driver is not especially cognizant of the paralleling dangers and so thinks nothing of just sitting right there next to my car. For them, being parallel to another car is no different than anything else about driving.

What I usually do in such a circumstance is I try to either slow down or speed-up and "break" the paralleling that is going on. Again, this is only when the situation presents itself and the paralleling is easily avoidable and there's no particular reason for the paralleling to be undertaken. Obviously, in a crowded freeway situation, trying to remain parallel-free is not readily performed.

In any case, we are developing AI that takes into account these ground rules of trying to avoid paralleling when feasible, along with being aware of the dangers when stuck with being in a parallel situation.

The AI seeks to anticipate that a paralleling situation is going to arise, and then how to deal with it. If there is a passing opportunity and the paralleling will occur by the overt act of the AI, the AI seeks to minimize the time and distance in which the paralleling will take place.

Thus, sometimes the AI is the instigator of the paralleling and sometimes it is merely the participant of a paralleling.

There are recurring patterns of traffic that through the use of Machine Learning (ML), and the use of deep learning and artificial neural networks, the AI can anticipate "good" versus "bad" acts of paralleling and act accordingly.

The AI needs to have programmatic capabilities that serve as the core of dealing with parallel situations, along with being augmented with driving tactics that are built around the use of large sets of traffic data and the use of ML.

AI developers need to consider wisely how to have the AI react to paralleling. If you opt to have the AI always maneuver away from a paralleling situation, the odds are that human drivers will figure this out. In that case, the savvy human drivers of cars nearby an AI self-driving might try to use this as a ploy to get an AI self-driving car to act in a manner that they want it to act. This is often referred to as pranking an AI self-driving car.

Another aspect of the paralleling involves the creepiness factor. Suppose you are driving your car and another car suddenly opts to stay parallel. Assuming that there is no particular driving reason for doing this, it could be that the other driver is essentially a creep.

Maybe they want to stare at you or stare at something else inside your car. As a driver, you would likely detect this, and I'd bet you'd pretty quickly try to get out of the situation. If the other car slows down as you slow down, or speeds up as you speed up, the creepiness factors gets even worse.

I've had situations that were creepy enough that I then opted to slow down and swing in behind the other car, hoping that then the other car would give up the stare aspects and just continue along.

In another case, I switched lanes and then even made a hasty exit from the freeway, doing so in a calculated manner that made it impossible for the other driver to also catch the same exit. You never know what might be in the mind of another driver and it is safest to find a means to avoid a confrontation.

There are road rage drivers that can let the smallest thing spark them into a danger mode.

The AI system can potentially even ask the human occupants of the self-driving car whether they might be bothered by a car that seems to keep paralleling the self-driving car.

Or, it could be that the human occupants of the self-driving car might alert the AI that there is another car that is eerily paralleling the AI self-driving car and ask that the AI do something about it.

This highlights the importance of Natural Language Processing (NLP) and the AI being able to converse with the human occupants in an AI self-driving car.

Are you watching your parallels while driving? Many drivers do not. They only give thought to the paralleling matter when it becomes readily apparent, such as trying to pass a large truck. Or, if you are trying to make a lane change and there's a car in the lane next to you and parallel to you, you are likely to give that car the evil eye and brainwave them to get out of your way.

For savvy AI that needs to properly drive a car, we don't believe that the paralleling aspects should be relegated to an obscure edge case or corner case, and instead it should be front-and-center as a vital capability of the AI driving system.

If anyone I know might be getting into an AI self-driving car, I would hope that the AI would be wise to dealing with parallel vehicles and try to ensure their safety accordingly. Come to think of it, I'd want anyone getting into an AI self-driving car to also be able to assume that the AI is versed in paralleling.

There is a mathematician's worn torn joke that parallel lines have so much in common that it is a shame that they will never meet.

In the case of AI self-driving cars, it is hoped that a self-driving car paralleling another vehicle will never "meet" the other vehicle (i.e., not smash into each other). The inches away dangers of paralleling another vehicle while in-motion needs to be a key to the AI driving tactics, and I'd say without hesitation that's no laughing matter.

CHAPTER 4
DEMENTIA DRIVERS
AND
AI SELF-DRIVING CARS

CHAPTER 4

DEMENTIA DRIVERS
AND AI SELF-DRIVING CARS

Do you know someone that seems to be progressively forgetting things and their mind cannot remain focused on matters at-hand? I'm not referring to the occasional moment whereby you might get distracted and misremember where you left your keys or where you put the TV remote.

We've likely all had those moments. I knew a friend in college that every time he noticed that someone else had lost something or misplaced an item, he would jump right away to the classic "have you lost your mind" and seemed to overplay the rather hackneyed phrase (it became an ongoing irritant to those of us that interacted with him regularly). It is easy to leap to foregone conclusions and falsely suggest that someone has a systemic mental failing.

Typically, regrettably, as we get older, humans do though tend to genuinely have a kind of mental decay and their brains sadly begin to deteriorate.

There are an estimated 5 million people in the United States that are currently experiencing dementia. To be clear, keep in mind that dementia is not a disease per se, though some assume it is, and instead it is considered an umbrella term that encompasses the loss of our thinking skills and also the degradation of various memory processing aspects. Dementia might start with no especially notable impairment and thus not be readily detectable and be easily shrugged off as

73

inconsequential. Gradually, dementia usually emerges as an increasingly persistent onset, which might then ultimately lead to becoming quite severe and debilitating for the person.

This decreasing capability of cognitive functioning can be tough for the person with it and also be tremendously trying for those that are around or connected with the person. Many people that experience dementia are quick to deny they have anything wrong with them at all.

It can be excruciatingly embarrassing and frightening to consider that you might have dementia. Some will do more than simply deny they have it and will attempt to showcase that they clearly do not suffer from it. In this effort to disprove the dementia, it often brings even more light to the dementia and perhaps illuminates it more so than others thought existed for the person.

I am reminded of the grandfather of a close friend of mine. My friend was grappling with his aging grandfather's behavior and actions that appeared to be symptomatic of dementia. The grandfather would get confused about the days and times that he was supposed to be taking medication for an ailment he had. He would forget the names of loved ones and could not identify their names when they came to visit him. I recall one time that I went to visit him, he brought me a cup of tea, and moments later he asked me if I wanted some tea. I pointed out I already had tea. Nonetheless, he went back to the kitchen and brought me another cup of tea.

Those kinds of cognitive failings were perhaps reasonably acceptable in the sense that they weren't preventing him from carrying on day-to-day and living a relatively normal existence. When the symptoms first began, my friend had "the talk" with him about dementia, which I'd say is more awkward than "the talk" of a father telling his son about the birds-and-the-bees. Having a son tell his own father that dementia is taking hold, well, it's something no one welcomes and likely everyone dreads.

Unfortunately, the dementia oozed into all other aspects of the grandfather's activities. Of which, the one that had perhaps had the most danger associated with it involved driving a car. The grandfather still had a legal driver's license. There was nothing legally that prevented him from driving a car. He owned a car. He had the keys to the car. He could freely use the car whenever he wished to do so. Indeed, he tied much of his sense of being to the use of the car. It was his path to freedom. He could drive to the store, or drive to the park, or drive any darned place that he wanted to get to.

I was over at the house with my friend when one day his grandfather announced that he was going for a drive. We watched as he slowly, very slowly, agonizingly slowly, backed out of the garage. As he did so, he also bumped into a child's bike that was stored in the garage.

Furthermore, he was turning the steering wheel as he backed out, which made no sense since the driveway was straight behind the car. He managed to get the car almost turned kitty-corner and it looked like he might drive onto the grass of the front yard. He barely corrected in time and ended-up slightly going off the curb, rather than the usual driveway cut that was amply provided.

He then backed further into the street, doing so at a pace that caused other oncoming cars to come to a halt and wait. It wasn't just a few brief seconds. It was somewhere around 30 seconds before he was able to fully get into the street, finally taking the car out of reverse, and put it into forward gear, and then eased down the road. I noticed that a neighbor's dog was off its leash and running around, including veering into the street. I don't believe the grandfather noticed the dog at all, and the car made no attempts to evade hitting the dog (luckily, the dog scampered on its own back to the grassy yards of the nearby homes).

If you are thinking why I am seemingly criticizing the grandfather about his driving, I'd like to emphasize that it is only because his driving skills had degraded and he was now becoming a danger to himself and others. I fully understand the importance he placed on personal mobility of having a car, along with the control, the emotional boost of driving, and so on. At some point we need to be equally thoughtful about the risk that his driving presents to his own well-being, and the well-being of others that come in contact with his car while he is driving.

Suppose he had hit that dog that was in the street? Suppose when backing out of the garage he had crushed the child's bike? Suppose as he cut across the grass toward the curb that a small child was there and got struck? Suppose that as he entered into the street, an ongoing car zipped along but he backed into it and caused a car accident. In all of these instances, he could have been injured or killed. He could have injured or killed others. He could have caused damage to property. Etc.

In addition to his memory loses and his cognitive processing loses, he was quite slow to mentally process things.

As you know, when driving a car, you are often confronted with situations that require a split-second kind of mental processing. Is that car going to run the red light, and if so, should you try to do an emergency braking or instead attempt to push on the gas and accelerate out of the situation? In his dementia, it was relatively apparent that he would not be able to make such decisions in the split seconds of time required. This further made his driving a kind of "menace" to the road (I hate to say it that way, but, we need to be honest about these matters, for safety's sake).

In all fairness, I also stipulate that sometimes there are situations wherein caring people inadvertently ascribe dementia to someone and their driving, when it has no such merit. My own now-adult-driver daughter still believes that I drive too slowly and conservatively. Do I have dementia? I don't think so, and nor does she assert it. But the point being that there are different kinds of driving styles and someone might have a different style that others don't like, but if it is still a fully lucid form of driving and one that exercises due safety and care, let's not just tarnish it with the dementia brush, so to speak.

In general, I would guess that we would all reasonably agree that if someone is hampered by dementia and it does so to the degree that it materially impairs their driving, the person ought to be reconsidering whether they should be driving or not.

I realize that in the case of the grandfather that he still actually had his driver's license, which you might insist "proves" that he can still sufficiently drive a car. Not really. It was instead more due to a formality in the sense that his driver's license had not come due for renewal involving a road-level driving test. Instead, he was just paying it for renewal year after year as a paperwork matter. This meant that the Department of Motor Vehicles (DMV) had no ready means to know that the grandfather was now an "impaired" driver.

I suppose you could say that if he was such a bad driver that he would have gotten a traffic ticket. And, if he had gotten a traffic ticket, the police would notify the DMV. Once the DMV was notified, certainly they would formally revoke his driver's license. Well, he drove just a few miles a couple of times a week and had done so in a town-like area that allowed his poor driving to not stick-out, and thus he didn't have any tickets as yet.

Would you prefer to wait until he actually hits someone or something, before we raise a red flag? I'd say that's trying to close the barn door after the horse has already gotten out.

Imagine how someone else would feel if they knew that you knew that the grandfather was unfit to drive a car, and yet the grandfather rammed into them or their children? Why didn't you take steps to prevent this from happening?

The kindness of letting someone with dementia to continue driving a car when it is unsafe to do so must be weighed against the dangers and damages the dementia-laden person can cause to other unsuspecting people and places by being behind-the-wheel. We all need to be mindful that a multi-ton vehicle can render life-or-death results when driven recklessly or irresponsibly, regardless of how sincere or well-meaning the driver might be in their heart.

What does this have to do with AI self-driving cars?

At the Cybernetic AI Self-Driving Car Institute, we are developing AI software for self-driving cars. One aspect involves the AI being able to discern or attempt to discern that other driver's on-the-road might be driving while suffering from severe dementia, and the AI should then take necessary driving precautions accordingly.

Allow me to elaborate.

I'd like to first clarify and introduce the notion that there are varying levels of AI self-driving cars. The topmost level is considered Level 5. A Level 5 self-driving car is one that is being driven by the AI and there is no human driver involved. For the design of Level 5 self-driving cars, the auto makers are even removing the gas pedal, brake pedal, and steering wheel, since those are contraptions used by human drivers. The Level 5 self-driving car is not being driven by a human and nor is there an expectation that a human driver will be present in the self-driving car. It's all on the shoulders of the AI to drive the car.

For self-driving cars less than a Level 5, there must be a human driver present in the car. The human driver is currently considered the responsible party for the acts of the car. The AI and the human driver are co-sharing the driving task. In spite of this co-sharing, the human is supposed to remain fully immersed into the driving task and be ready at all times to perform the driving task. I've repeatedly warned about the dangers of this co-sharing arrangement and predicted it will produce many untoward results.

Let's focus herein on the true Level 5 self-driving car. Much of the comments apply to the less than Level 5 self-driving cars too, but the fully autonomous AI self-driving car will receive the most attention in this discussion.

Here's the usual steps involved in the AI driving task:

- Sensor data collection and interpretation

- Sensor fusion

- Virtual world model updating

- AI action planning

- Car controls command issuance

Another key aspect of AI self-driving cars is that they will be driving on our roadways in the midst of human driven cars too. There are some pundits of AI self-driving cars that continually refer to a Utopian world in which there are only AI self-driving cars on the public roads. Currently there are about 250+ million conventional cars in the United States alone, and those cars are not going to magically disappear or become true Level 5 AI self-driving cars overnight.

Indeed, the use of human driven cars will last for many years, likely many decades, and the advent of AI self-driving cars will occur while there are still human driven cars on the roads. This is a crucial point since this means that the AI of self-driving cars needs to be able to contend with not just other AI self-driving cars, but also contend with human driven cars. It is easy to envision a simplistic and rather unrealistic world in which all AI self-driving cars are politely interacting with each other and being civil about roadway interactions. That's not what is going to be happening for the foreseeable future. AI self-driving cars and human driven cars will need to be able to cope with each other.

Returning to the topic of dementia driving, the AI of a self-driving car ought to be imbued with an ability to assess other drivers and whether or not they are driving in a "safe and sane" manner. Since the AI cannot somehow reach into the mind of human drivers that are on-the-road, the AI must observe the behavior of the car and infer from that observable behavior the likely state-of-mind of the human driver.

Presumably, if there's a car up ahead that is another AI self-driving car, the AI of the AI self-driving car behind it does not need to worry as much about the AI driven car as it would of a human driven car. Some AI developers would argue that the AI of one self-driving car should actually have zero worries and zero need to observe another AI self-driving car, since the other AI self-driving car is going to always do the right thing and not make any errors that a human driver might make (so these AI developers would claim).

This perspective by some AI developers is what I refer to as an idealistic view, which I sometimes also describe as an egocentric design view.

Let's acknowledge that once we get to true Level 5 self-driving cars, not all of the respective AI's will be the same. Different auto makers and different tech firms will have developed different kinds of AI systems for their own proprietary self-driving car models. As such, each AI self-driving car model that comes from different auto makers will act and react in different ways from each other.

Furthermore, since there will be different AI's, there will be likely different ways of driving, and the AI of one self-driving car ought to be watching out for the behaviors of the AI of other self-driving cars.

That being said, I certainly concede that presumably the AI of another AI self-driving car is supposed to ultimately be more reliable, more consistent, more prone to proper driving than would be human drivers. Let me make clear that I am not suggesting that the AI only observe other AI self-driving cars, and somehow not observe human driven cars too.

I am instead clarifying and emphasizing that for those that assume the AI would only try to observe human driven cars for driving behavior, I'd argue that's insufficient and the AI should also be observing the other AI driven cars too.

Fortunately, it will likely be easier for one AI self-driving car to directly communicate with another AI self-driving car, since they will hopefully be using in-common V2V (vehicle-to-vehicle) electronic communications. This would make things easier in the sense that the AI of one self-driving car might ask another AI as to why it just suddenly and unexpectedly changed lanes ahead, which maybe the other AI might reply that there is debris in the lane ahead and thus it then explains the seemingly odd behavior and also aids the other AI in avoiding the same debris.

Imagine if we humans were all using our cell phones while driving and continually conversing with each other. Hey you, in the red sports car ahead, why did you make that crazy right turn? Though this might be a means to aid traffic, it could also spark quite a bit of road rage. No more needing to just raise your finger to make a statement to another driver, you could speak with them directly. I'd dare say our roads would turn into boxing matches. It wouldn't be pretty.

In any case, let's get back to the notion that the AI of your self-driving car will be observing the behavior of other cars. Doing so will aid the AI in trying to anticipate or predict what the other car might next do. By being able to make insightful predictions, the AI of your self-driving car will have a chance at being a better defensive driver and avoid untoward incidents. The AI will also be able to line-up evasive actions when needed, doing so before there is insufficient time left to react to an emerging dire situation.

What kinds of telltale clues might a dementia-laden driver provide?

Here's some that we train our AI to be on the look for:

- Riding of the brakes as exhibited by continual brake lights or slowing inexplicably
- Pumping of the brakes repeatedly even though there is no apparent reason to do so
- Signaling to make a right turn and then making no turn or making a left turn
- Signaling to make a left turn and then making no turn or making a right turn
- Turn signal continuously on for no apparent reason since no turning action is arising
- Rolls through a stop sign
- Speeds-up, slows down, speeds-up, slows down, but not due to traffic conditions
- Not driving in a defensive manner and gets stuck or trapped in obvious traffic predicaments
- Runs a red light
- Comes to a halt in traffic when there is no apparent cause
- Makes attempts at exits or turns and then suddenly reverts away from the attempt
- Veers into the emergency lane or bike lane and no apparent cause to do so
- Nearly hits other cars or pedestrians or roadway objects
- Goes radically slower than the rest of traffic
- Goes radically faster than the rest of traffic
- Other cars are having to get out of the way of the observed car

- Other cars honk their horns at the observed car or make other untoward motions

- Keeps changing lanes when there is no apparent reason to do so

- Cuts off other cars when changing lanes and making other maneuvers

- Other

Please make sure to review this dementia-laden driving symptoms list with a grain of salt. I am sure all of us have performed one or more of those kinds of driving actions from time-to-time. Maybe you are groggy from that late-night partying and in the morning your driving is not at your usual peak performance. Maybe you are in a foul mood and taking it out on the rest of the traffic. Plus, novice teenage driver often performs those same moves, primarily because they are still wrestling with the basics of driving and aren't sure of what they are doing.

The notion is that any of those driving actions in isolation could be due to any number of reasons.

I once had a bee that got into my car while I was driving, and I regrettably weaved across the lanes as I was trying to get the scary critter out of my car. A momentary act that appears out of the ordinary should be construed as a potential warning that perhaps the driver is somehow amiss, but it usually takes more than one single act to fully make it onto the "watch out for that car" mindset (unless the single act is so egregious that it is clear cut that something bad is happening).

You might be wondering what the big deal is about detecting a car that has these kinds of foul driving actions?

The odds are that once you spot this kind of behavior emerging, it will likely continue if the driver has some systemic issues involved in their driving. This gives the AI a heads-up to be especially wary of that car.

For example, if the AI detected that a car ahead was needlessly riding its brakes, this might be a sign that the driver might soon take some other dangerous action such as a wild turn or veering into other lanes. The AI would then anticipate this possibility and potentially change the path of the self-driving car. It might be safer to route to another road or perhaps let the car ahead get some distance between the AI self-driving car and it. These are all prudent defensive driving actions by the AI and would be spurred when a car appears to be driven in an untoward manner.

Some of you might be saying that these kinds of driving moves could be undertaken by a drunk driver. You are indeed right! I would suggest that a drunk driver could do any or all of those kinds of driving moves. A drunk driver might do those and even go further and make even worse moves. Can you for sure distinguish between a drunk driver and a dementia-laden driver, based on the behavior exhibited by the car's actions? It is hard to assert that you could make such a distinction without otherwise scrutinizing the actual human driver to figure out what is afoot.

If an AI self-driving car is able to detect a potential dementia-laden driver, it could try to alert other nearby AI self-driving cars about the matter. Using the V2V, the AI might send a message to be on-the-watch for a blue sedan that is at the corner of Main and Sprout street and heading west. Other AI self-driving cars would then be able to likewise be prepared for evasive action. There is even the possibility of using a swarm-like approach to provide a safety driving traffic cocoon for the driver.

I realize that this seems a bit like Big Brother to have other cars watching for and then taking semi-collective action about another driver that is on-the-road. I would claim though that this already happens to some extent with human drivers acting at times in a collective manner.

In the case of the grandfather, the other drivers in the neighborhood knew that he was a driver that was increasingly getting worse and worse. They would often "shield" his driving by purposely driving near to him and helping to clear traffic nearby. It was almost like a parade of cars, but the "star" of the parade was not even aware that his fellow neighbors were taking such an action (which reinforces that his dementia was bad enough that he couldn't discern what the other traffic was doing for him).

Some drivers that have dementia will at least try to minimize their chances of getting themselves into trouble. For example, if they have an especially difficult time when driving in a location they do not know, they will drive only on streets they do know. If they have a difficult time comprehending traffic at nighttime, they will purposely only drive during daylight. If they know that lots of other traffic confounds them, they'll wait until the least traffic periods to then get onto the roadway. Etc.

Ultimately, if the dementia overtakes the ability to appropriately drive a car, something will need to be done to ensure that the person does not get behind a wheel. The so-called "taking away the keys" has got to be one of the hardest acts to undertake. It is hard for the person that is forfeiting their keys and the privilege of driving. It is hard for whomever has to take away the keys. The matter can create ill will and taint the rest of the person's existence.

The good news is that with the advent of true Level 5 self-driving cars, it is anticipated that those with dementia will still be able to have the mobility they crave, simply by using AI self-driving cars to get them where they want to go.

Sure, they won't be able to get behind the wheel of the car, but I think they'll accept the notion of being a passenger rather than a driver, particularly due to the aspect that lots and lots of other people will be doing so too.

In other words, those people getting into AI self-driving cars will include many that could drive if they wished, and instead they prefer to let the driving be done by the AI self-driving car. The person with dementia won't standout as someone using an AI self-driving car since we'll all be routinely using AI self-driving cars.

Family members and friends are usually the first to realize that someone is succumbing to dementia. Allowing an untoward driver onto the roadways is nearly the same as letting a drunk driver onto the road. Most of us would likely try to stop someone that is drunk from getting behind the wheel. It's easier of course to do so since it is likely a one-time stopping action and not something of a more permanent nature.

The person with dementia will eventually reach a crossover point that makes their driving dangerous for themselves and dangerous for everyone else.

Hopefully, if you do need to intervene and take away the keys, the advent of AI self-driving cars will have become so pervasive that their shifting into a ridesharing mode of using AI self-driving cars will ease the agony of losing the privilege to drive a car.

Since we will have a mixture of both human driven cars and AI self-driving cars for a long time, you'll unfortunately still need to be ready to be the gatekeeper of dealing with the key's removal aspects.

In any case, the AI of the self-driving car has to be savvy enough to be watchful for dementia-laden drivers and take the kinds of evasive actions to save the lives of those intertwined in traffic with that untoward driver. I think we can all agree we'd want the AI to be watchful and have the capability to contend with these potentially life-and-death matters.

CHAPTER 5
AUGMENTED REALTY (AR)
AND
AI SELF-DRIVING CARS

CHAPTER 5

AUGMENTED REALTY (AR)
AND AI SELF-DRIVING CARS

When I was initially showing my teenagers how to drive a car, we would go over to the local mall after-hours and use the nearly empty parking lot as an area to do some test driving. Round and round we would go, circling throughout the vast parking lot. Having a novice teenage driver at the wheel can be rather chilling due to their newness at steering and guiding a multi-ton vehicle that can readily crash into things.

Fortunately, the parking lot had very few obstacles and so the need to be especially accurate in where the car went was not as crucial in comparison to being on a conventional street (or, imagine being in the mall during open hours, which we later tried too, and it was a near heart attack kind of moment).

Once they got comfortable with driving any which way in the empty mall parking lot, I would up the game by asking them to pretend that there were cars in the parking stalls.

Each stall was marked by white painted lines on the asphalt, so it was relatively easy to imagine where the parked cars would be. While driving up and down the rows of pretend parked cars, if they veered over a painted white line, I'd then tell them that they just hit a car. At first, I was repeatedly having to say this. Hey, you just hit a Volvo. Ouch, you just rammed into a Mercedes. And so on.

Eventually, they were able to navigate the mall parking lot rather cleanly. No more ramming of pretend cars. I then had them practice parking in a parking stall or slot. I'd insist that they pretend that there was a car to the left and a car to the right of the parking spot and thus they would need to enter into the spot without scratching against those adjacent cars. We did this for a while and gradually they were able to pull into a parking stall and back-out of it without touching any of the pretend cars.

Having perfected driving throughout the essentially empty mall parking lot, and being able to park at will, I then asked them to pretend that there were other obstacles to be dealt with. We were near a Macy's department store and I explained that they were to pretend that shoppers were flowing out of the store into the parking lot to get to their cars, and likewise people were parking their cars so they could go into the store. I would point with my fingers and tell them that there was a person here and there, and over there, and one that is walking next to the car. Etc.

This was a much harder kind of pretend. I would tell them they just hit a pedestrian that was trying to get quickly to their car, but we'd have a debate about where the "person" really was. I was accused of magically making people appear in places as though they just instantaneously were beamed to earth, rather than having had a chance to spot a person walking slowly through the parking lot as would happen in real-life. This attempt to create a more populated and complex virtual world was becoming difficult for both me and the learning drivers, so I gave up trying to use that method for their test driving.

Let's now shift in time and cover a seemingly different topic, but I think you'll catch-on as to why I am doing so.

Unless you were living in a cave in July 2016, you likely knew then or know now about the release of Pokémon Go. The Pokémon game had long been popular and especially my own kids relished the Pokémon merchandise and shows. Pokémon Go is an app for your smartphone that makes use of Augmented Reality (AR) to layer Pokémon characters onto the real-world. You hold-up your smartphone and turn-on the camera, and lo-and-behold you are suddenly able to see your favorite Pokémon strutting in front of you, or standing over next to a building, or climbing up a pole.

You are supposed to try and find and capture the various virtual characters. This prompted many people to wander around their neighborhoods searching the real-world and the virtual-world to locate prized Pokémon. Some suggested that this was a boon for getting especially younger people off-their-duffs and getting outdoors for some exercise. Rather than sitting in a room and continually playing an online game, they now had to walk around and be immersed in the outdoors. It also was a potential social energizer due to getting multiples of people to gather together to jointly search for the virtual characters.

Unfortunately, it also has had some downsides. There were some players of the game that got themselves into rather questionable situations. If they saw a character perched on the edge of a cliff, they might accidentally be so hot in the pursuit of the character that they themselves fell off the cliff. There were stories of players wandering into bad neighborhoods and getting mugged, and supposedly in some cases muggers waiting in hiding since they knew that people would come to them via pursuit of the virtual characters.

There were reports too that some people became so transfixed in looking at their smartphones to try and spot the virtual characters that they would accidently walk into obstacles. You might be riveting your attention to chasing a Pokémon that you failed to see the fire hydrant ahead of you and thus you tripped over it.

Or, some pursued a Pokémon out into the street and got nearly run over by a car. What makes this particularly vexing is that the car driver does not know why you are suddenly running into the street in front of their car. It would be one thing if you had a dog and it got loose, and you opted to chase after the dog into the street. The car driver could likely see the dog and have predicted that someone might try to run after it. In the case of the virtual world on your smartphone, the car driver has no idea that you are avidly pursuing a Pikachu (a popular Pokémon character) and therefore the driver might be taken aback that someone has blindly stepped into the path of the car.

I'll now tie together my first story about the mall parking lot driving with the story about Pokémon Go.

Back when I was helping my teenagers learn to drive, Augmented Reality was still being established and it was relatively crude and a computer cycles hog. The advent of having AR on a smartphone that could update in near real-time was a sign that AR was finally becoming something that could touch the masses and not be only relegated to very expensive goggles.

During my teaching moments about driving a car, I had dreamed that it would be handy to have a Heads-up Display (HUD) on the car that would make use of a virtual-world overlay on the real-world so that I could do more than just pretend in our minds that there were various obstacles in the parking lot. I would have liked to have the entire front windshield of the car act like a portal that would continue to show the real-world, and yet also allow an overlay of a virtual world.

If I could have done so, I would have then had a computer portray people walking throughout the parking lot. It could also have presented cars in the parking stalls. Since the virtual world would involve animation and movement, I would have virtualized "pretend" cars that were backing out of parking spots, some might be trying to pull into parking spots, others might be meandering around the mall searching for a parking spot.

Just think of how rich an experience this could have been. There we would be in a nearly empty parking lot, and yet by using the windshield to also portray the made-up virtual world, my teenager drivers would actually see pedestrians, other cars, perhaps shopping carts, and a myriad of other objects that would be in a real-world real parking lot.

Furthermore, I would presumably be able to adjust the complexity of the virtual portrayals. I might start by having just a few pedestrians and a few cars, and then after my teenage drivers got used to this situation, I could have made the parking lot seem like the crazed shopping day of Black Friday encompassing zillions of people and cars filling the mall parking lot. With just a few keystrokes the surrounding driving environment could be adjusted and allow for a wide variety of scenarios and testing circumstances.

The beauty too of this virtual world overlay would be that if the novice driver happened to hit an AR portrayed car or pedestrian, no one was actually injured or killed. I'm not saying that their hitting any such AR presented artifact would be good, but at least it is better to have it happen in a virtual sense and presumably avert ever doing so in the real-world sense.

I might even have purposely used a no-win scenario wherein they would be forced into hitting something or someone, doing so to get them to a realization of the seriousness of driving a car. It is one thing to generally know that you could hit someone or something but doing it even in a virtual sense would seem to hammer home the dangers involved in driving. By the way, allow me to clarify that my kids have always been serious and thoughtful drivers and I'm quite thankful for that!

The use of Augmented Reality related to cars has increasingly become a thing, as they say. There are indeed prototype and experimental windshields that will now do the kind of virtual world overlay that I've been depicting. These tend to be expensive and more so a research effort than something deployed into everyday use. Nonetheless, great strides are being made in this realm.

Why would you use a HUD in your car with AR? If you are worried that this might lend itself to playing Pokémon Go while actively driving a car, let's hope that's not what emerges. The idea instead is that the car itself might use its own sensors to help you with comprehending the driving scene ahead of you. If the car is equipped with cameras it might be able to identify in the scene ahead where cars are, where pedestrians are, where the street signs are, and so on. The windshield would then have virtualized circles and outlines that would point out those real-world objects.

I'm sure you've been driving and tried to find a street sign so that you would know the name of the street you are on, or maybe to see what the speed limit is. Sometimes those signs can be hard to quickly spot, especially when you are driving the car and mainly trying to watch the street traffic. Via the car sensors, a computer might be able to find the street signs and when you are looking out your windshield it would have say red outlines that surround each of the nearby street signs. This would then give you a quick visual nudge as to where the street signs are.

Another aspect could be the computer predicting where traffic is going to go next. Suppose you are driving your car and have come up to an intersection. You are waiting to make a left turn. Another car is approaching from the other side of the street. The AR could show a visual arrow on your windshield pointing to where that car is going to go, and you would then be aided by the computer having forewarned you about the upcoming car. It might make a difference in that you could have possibly not realized the car would intercept your intended path, and yet via the windshield HUD it is now portrayed right there in front of your eyes.

One significant criticism of the AR overlay onto a windshield is that it could be as much a distractor as a helper. Maybe when the AR overlay is showing you where the street signs are, it causes your attention to shift toward looking at the street signs and you miss seeing the bicyclist coming up from your left. The use of a HUD can be both a blessing and a curse. In many respects it could boost your driving capabilities and help make you a safer driver. In other ways it could undermine your driving capabilities and cause you to take your eye off the ball. This is an open debate and still being argued about.

There are other emerging AR uses for cars too.

Remember the car owner's manual that presumably came with your car? It probably sits in your glove compartment and you rarely take it out to look at it. Some auto makers are using AR to make your owner's manual more engaging and hopefully more useful. You download their app on your smartphone and then open the camera and point it at the owner's manual. When you turn the pages of the owner's manual, the AR will overlay additional information and animation.

Suppose that the owner's manual explains how to adjust the settings on your complicated in-car stereo and radio entertainment system. The manual might have a series of pictures and a narrative explaining how to make adjustments to the entertainment system. This can be confusing though as you look at the manual and look at your actual car, trying to figure out how the flat and unmoving pictures in the owner's manual are equivalent to what you see in front of you as you are seated in the driver's seat. Via the AR, the owner's manual might "come alive" and show animation of adjusting the entertainment system. This could make things easier for you to understand what to do.

Even more immersive is the use of the AR to hold-up your smartphone and aim it at the dashboard where your entertainment system controls reside. The owner's manual is now overlaid to the real-world dashboard. It can then show you exactly where the controls are and how to adjust them. In that sense, you don't even need a paper-based owner's manual per se and can just use the online version that also has the AR capability included too.

Another use of AR by auto makers involves trying to sell you are a car.

You are at the car dealership and looking at the car model they have sitting in the dealership showroom. It is red in color and has conventional tires. You download an app and turn-on the AR, and upon holding up your smartphone to point it at the car, you indicate to the app to "change" the color from red to blue. Voila, suddenly the car in the showroom is blue instead of red. You also are considering the super-traction tires in lieu of the conventional tires, and so you instruct the AR to "change" the tires accordingly. You are now looking at your desired car and can feel more comfortable that it will be what you actually want to purchase.

For the marketing of cars, you could download an AR app from an auto maker and hold-up your smartphone to look at the street in your neighborhood, and by doing so you suddenly see their brand of car driving down your street. It is a virtual depiction of their brand of car. You then think of yourself behind the wheel and driving down your street, the envy of your neighbors. Might just entice you to go ahead and buy that car (well, buy it for real, not an imaginary version).

What does this have to do with AI self-driving cars?

At the Cybernetic AI Self-Driving Car Institute, we are developing AI software for self-driving cars. One emerging means to try and test AI self-driving cars involves the use of Augmented Reality.

Allow me to elaborate.

I'd like to first clarify and introduce the notion that there are varying levels of AI self-driving cars. The topmost level is considered Level 5. A Level 5 self-driving car is one that is being driven by the AI and there is no human driver involved. For the design of Level 5 self-driving cars, the auto makers are even removing the gas pedal, brake pedal, and steering wheel, since those are contraptions used by human drivers. The Level 5 self-driving car is not being driven by a human and nor is there an expectation that a human driver will be present in the self-driving car. It's all on the shoulders of the AI to drive the car.

For self-driving cars less than a Level 5, there must be a human driver present in the car. The human driver is currently considered the responsible party for the acts of the car. The AI and the human driver are co-sharing the driving task. In spite of this co-sharing, the human is supposed to remain fully immersed into the driving task and be ready at all times to perform the driving task. I've repeatedly warned about the dangers of this co-sharing arrangement and predicted it will produce many untoward results.

Let's focus herein on the true Level 5 self-driving car. Much of the comments apply to the less than Level 5 self-driving cars too, but the fully autonomous AI self-driving car will receive the most attention in this discussion.

Here's the usual steps involved in the AI driving task:
- Sensor data collection and interpretation
- Sensor fusion
- Virtual world model updating
- AI action planning
- Car controls command issuance

Another key aspect of AI self-driving cars is that they will be driving on our roadways in the midst of human driven cars too. There are some pundits of AI self-driving cars that continually refer to a utopian world in which there are only AI self-driving cars on the public roads. Currently there are about 250+ million conventional cars in the United States alone, and those cars are not going to magically disappear or become true Level 5 AI self-driving cars overnight.

Indeed, the use of human driven cars will last for many years, likely many decades, and the advent of AI self-driving cars will occur while there are still human driven cars on the roads. This is a crucial point since this means that the AI of self-driving cars needs to be able to contend with not just other AI self-driving cars, but also contend with human driven cars. It is easy to envision a simplistic and rather unrealistic world in which all AI self-driving cars are politely interacting with each other and being civil about roadway interactions. That's not what is going to be happening for the foreseeable future. AI self-driving cars and human driven cars will need to be able to cope with each other.

Returning to the topic of Augmented Reality and AI self-driving cars, let's consider the matter of testing of AI self-driving cars and see how AR might be of help.

Testing of AI self-driving cars is one of the most worrisome and controversial topics in the AI self-driving car arena.

Here's the fundamental question for you: How should AI of self-driving cars be tested?

I'll help you answer the question by providing these various ways that you could do the testing of the AI of a self-driving car:

- Test the AI software in-absence of being in the actual car and do what some people refer to as bench testing.

- Test the AI software via the use of simulations that act as though the AI is driving in a real-world setting.

- Test the AI software while "in silicio" (Latin meaning in silicon, while actually on-board of the self-driving car) on a closed test track that is purposely established for testing cars.

- Testing the AI software while on-board and on public roads in some constrained manner such as a particular geofenced portion of a town or city.

- Testing the AI software while on-board and on public roads in an unconstrained manner such that the AI self-driving car travels to anyplace that a conventional car might travel to.

- Other

One quick answer to my question about where should an AI self-driving be tested is that you could say "All of the Above" since it would seem potentially prudent to try each of the aforementioned approaches. There is no one particular testing approach that is the "best" per se and each of the approaches has trade-offs.

There are some critics of the latter ways of testing involving putting the AI self-driving car onto public roads. It is viewed by some that until AI self-driving cars are "perfected" they should not be allowed onto public roads at all. This seems sensible in that if you are putting an untested or shall we say partially tested AI self-driving car onto public roads, you are presumably putting people and anything else on the public roads into greater risk if the AI self-driving car goes awry.

Proponents of public road testing argue that we will never have any fully tested AI self-driving cars until they are allowed to be on public roads. This is due to the wide variety of driving situations that can be encountered on public roads and for which the other methods of testing generally perhaps cannot equally match. A test track can only undertake so many differing kinds of tests. It is akin to driving in a mall parking lot, of sorts, though of course much more extensive, but in comparison to the public roads approach it is considered quite constrained and limited.

Do you confine AI self-driving cars to being tested solely via only non-public roads testing and wait until this has tested every possible permutation and combination (which many would argue is not especially feasible), or do you let AI self-driving cars onto the public roads to try and make ready progress toward the advent of AI self-driving cars? This would be a kind of risk-reward proposition. Some say that if you don't allow the public roads option, you might either not have AI self-driving cars for many decades to come, or you might not ever be satisfied with AI self-driving cars even via their other testing method and thus doom AI self-driving cars to never seeing the light of day, as it were.

To try and reduce the risks associated with putting AI self-driving cars onto public roads for testing, the auto makers and tech firms have opted to usually include a human back-up driver in the AI self-driving car. In theory, this implies that the risks of the AI self-driving car going awry are minimized due to the notion that the back-up driver will take over the controls when needed. I've mentioned many times that the human back-up driver should not be construed as a silver bullet solution to this matter and that human back-up drivers are merely an added layer of protection but not a foolproof instrument.

If you think about the testing of AI self-driving cars in terms of number of miles driven, it is a means to try and grapple with the magnitude of the testing problem.

Various studies have tried to identify how many miles an AI self-driving car would need to drive to be able to presumably encounter a relatively complete range and diversity of driving conditions, and also do so without presumably getting involved in any incidents so as to suggest that it has now become sufficiently capable to be considered "safe" (depending on your definition of the word "safe").

This also raises other questions such as what constitutes an incident. If an AI self-driving bumps against another car but there is no material damage, and no one was hurt, does that constitute an incident or do we let it slide? Should we only consider incidents to be those that involve human injury? What about fatalities and how should those be weighed versus incidents involving injuries that are non-fatal?

There is also the matter of whether or not the AI self-driving car is "learning" during the time that it is driving. If so, you then have a somewhat moving goalpost in terms of the number of driving miles needed. Suppose the AI self-driving car goes X number of miles without any incident, it then has a serious incident, but it presumably "learns" or is somehow adjusted so that it will not once again get involved in such an incident. Do you now restart the clock, so to speak, and scrap the prior miles of driving as now water under the bridge, and say that the AI self-driving car has to now go Y number of miles to prove itself to be somehow error free?

I'd like to also clarify that this prevalent notion in the media of "zero fatalities" once we truly have AI self-driving cars is a rather questionable suggestion. If a pedestrian suddenly steps into the street and in front of an oncoming car, whether driven by a human or by AI, and if there is insufficient stopping distance, there is nothing magical about the AI that will make the car suddenly disappear or leap over the pedestrian. We are going to have fatalities even with the Utopian world of only AI self-driving cars.

In any case, on the driving miles question, some studies suggest we might need to have AI self-driving cars that have driven billions of miles, perhaps 5 to 10 billion as a placeholder, before we might all feel comfortable that sufficient testing has taken place. That suggests we would have some number of AI self-driving cars on public roads for billions of miles. Keep in mind that this road-time is during the "testing" phase of the AI self-driving car, and not once the testing is already completed.

Meanwhile, Google's Waymo is way out in front of the other AI self-driving car makers by having accumulated by their reported numbers to be somewhere around 10 million driving miles. For those of you that are statistics minded, you might realize that 10 million is only 1% of 1 billion, and thus this makes evident that if billions of miles are the goal that even the front runner is a far cry from reaching that number.

With the use of simulations, which I had mentioned earlier as a potential testing method, it is obviously relatively easy to do large-scale driving miles since there is not any actual rubber meeting the road. You can crank up the computer cycles and do as many miles of simulations as you can afford on your computer. There are some that are using or intend to use super-computers to ramp-up the complexity and the driving volumes of their simulations.

Waymo has variously reported that they have surpassed around 5 billion miles of simulation testing. They continue to crank away at the use of the simulations while also having their self-driving cars on the roadways.

This illustrates my earlier point that doing testing is likely to involve using some or all of the testing methods that I've listed. I would also add that some view the testing methods as being serial and to be done in a set sequence. Thus, you would presumably do all of your simulation testing, finish it, and then move toward putting your self-driving car on the roads. Others point out that this is a less effective method and that you need to undertake the various testing approaches simultaneously. This particularly arises regarding how to best setup the simulation, which I'll further describe in a moment.

There are some that say that simulated miles are not all equal. By this they are meaning that it all depends upon how you've setup your simulation and whether it is truly representative of a real-world driving environment. Someone could setup a simulation involving driving around and around in a tight circle and then run it for billions of miles of a simulated AI self-driving car trying to drive in that circle. Besides the AI self-driving car maybe getting dizzy, it would give us little faith that the AI self-driving car has been sufficiently tested.

I don't think any of the serious auto makers or tech firms developing AI self-driving cars are setting up their simulations in this rudimentary circling-only way. But it does bring up the valid point that the simulation does need to be complex enough to likely match to the real-world. This is also why doing more than one testing method at a time can be handy. If your AI self-driving car encounters a situation in the real-world, you can use that as a "lesson learned" and adjust your simulation to include that situation and other such situations that are sparked by the instance.

The biggest and easiest criticism or considered weakness of the simulation as a testing method is that it is not the same as having a real self-driving car that is driving on real roads. A lot of people would be hesitant to have full faith and belief that a simulated run is sufficient all on its own. How do you know that the simulation accurately even modeled the AI self-driving car? The odds are that the simulation does not necessarily have the AI running on the same actual hardware as found in the self-driving car. It is more likely that it is running as part of the simulation. The simulation is regrettably likely not the same as the actual AI sitting on-board the AI self-driving car and "experiencing" the driving environment as it is so experienced when an actual car is actually on actual roads.

We then ought to take a look at the test track approach. It involves the actual AI self-driving car on an actual road. The rub is that the closed tracks are only so many acres in size. They can only offer so many variations of driving situations. Furthermore, if you want to have the testing involve real people to be pedestrians or driving other cars nearby the AI self-driving car, you need to hire people to do so, and they are potentially put into harms way if you are going to try some risky maneuvers such as a pedestrian that darts into the street in front of the AI self-driving car or have a human driven car that tries to dangerously cut-off the AI self-driving car.

A test track would need to be well-equipped with street lights, intersections, bike lanes, traffic signals, sidewalks, and a slew of other infrastructure and obstacles that we face on public roads. The question then arises as to how many testing situations can you devise? What is the cost to setup and have an actual AI self-driving car undertake the test? You are not going to be seeking to drive millions or billions of miles on the closed track and so instead need to setup specific scenarios that come to mind.

Another factor is the familiarity aspects that an AI self-driving car might "learn" on a closed track. If the AI self-driving car is used repeatedly in the same confined space, it will presumably over time begin to "memorize" aspects of it. This might color the nature of the testing. Will the AI self-driving car when confronted anew with variants of the setup, once released onto public roads, be able to adequately cope with the fresh settings of the public roads in comparison to the repeated settings of the closed track?

It is like a baby duckling that imprints on a dog rather than an adult duck. What will the duckling be able to do when wandering in a large scope world of other ducks?

I'll also mention as an aside that the same question about repeated runs is similarly mentioned about the public roads efforts of testing in constrained ways. If you geofence an AI self-driving car to a set of city blocks and it repeatedly drives only in those city blocks, you are getting hopefully really good proficiency in that geofenced area, but you have to ask whether this is then going to be truly generalized to other locales. It could be that the AI self-driving car only is able to sufficiently drive in the geofenced area, but once allowed to roam further will get confused or not be able to respond as quickly due to being in a fresh area. This is often referred to as prevalence-induced behavior.

We are faced with the conundrum that each of the testing methods has their own respective upsides and downsides. As mentioned, you can still aim to try each of the methods, though you would want to be aware of their respective limitations and act accordingly. Furthermore, you would want to make sure that whatever is learned from one method is fed into the other methods. I want to emphasize I am not just saying that you would adjust or improve the AI self-driving car by learning from the other testing methods. You would also want to adjust or improve the other respective testing methods based on learnings from the other testing methods.

If a public roads testing in a constrained setting revealed something of interest, besides potentially adjusting or improving the AI for the on-board self-driving car, you would likely also want to adjust the simulation accordingly too. And, if you were doing closed track testing, you might want to hone in on the public roads reveal to then use it in the closed track setting. They each would infuse the other.

What role might Augmented Reality play in this?

Suppose we could add Augmented Reality into the closed track testing. The twist is that we don't need to do a Heads-up Display (HUD) approach per se since there isn't a human driver in a Level 5 self-driving car (I'm excluding for the moment a potential back-up human driver). Instead, what we could do is try to convince the AI on-board the self-driving car that there are things in the test track that aren't really there. We would merge together a virtual world with the real-world of the test track.

The cameras on the AI self-driving car are receiving images and video that depict what the self-driving car can "see" around it. Suppose we intercepted those images and video and added some virtual world aspects into it. We might put an image of a pedestrian standing at the crosswalk and waiting to cross at the test track intersection. This is not an actual human pedestrian. It is a made-up image of a pedestrian. This made-up imaginary pedestrian is overlaid onto the real-world scene that the AI self-driving car is being fed.

The AI self-driving car is essentially "fooled" into getting images that include a pedestrian, and therefore we can test to see if the AI is able to interpret the images and realize that a pedestrian is standing there. There is no risk to an actual human pedestrian because there is none standing there. There is no cost involved in hiring a person to stand there. We dispense with the logistics of having to deal with getting someone to come and pretend to be a pedestrian on the test track.

Keep in mind that we are not doing a simulation of the AI self-driving car at this point -- the AI is running on the actual AI self-driving car which is actually there on the actual test track. The only "simulated" aspects at this juncture would be the pedestrian at the corner. They are the simulated aspect which has now been merged into the "perceived" real-world environment.

Here's how the AI self-driving car would normally do things:

- Camera captures images and video (the AI has not yet seen it)

- It is fed to the AI

- The AI analyzes the captured images and video to see what's there

- The AI updates the internal model of what is around the self-driving car accordingly

- The AI assesses the internal model to determine what actions to take in driving the car

Here's the way it might work with the AR included:

- Camera captures images and video (the AI has not yet seen it)

- NEW: The captured images and video are fed into the AR special app

- NEW: The AR special app analyzes the images and video and inserts a pedestrian at the corner

- NEW: The AR special app now feeds the AR-augmented images and video into the AI

- The AI analyzes the captured images and video to see what's there

- The AI updates the internal model of what is around the self-driving car accordingly

- The AI assesses the internal model to determine what actions to take in driving the car

The AR becomes an interloper that grabs the images and videos, adds the virtual world elements, and then feeds this into the AI of the self-driving car.

From the perspective of the AI in the self-driving car, it has no indication that the images and videos were not otherwise collected in raw from the sensors. This allows then appropriate testing of the AI, since if we had to change the AI to be able cope with this AR augmentation, we would then have a "different" version of the AI than would normally be in the AI self-driving car that we are intending to put onto public roads (which, I might point out, could be another way to do this, though with my caveat as mentioned that it will then differ from what presumably is on the roadways).

What could you include then into the virtual world that you are going to "trick" the AI self-driving car that's on the closed track to believe exists there on the closed track?

You can have just about anything you might want. There could be virtual people, such as pedestrians and bicyclists. There could be virtual objects such as tree that falls in front of the AI self-driving car, but there isn't an actual tree and it just a made-up one. There could be virtual infrastructure such as added traffic signals that aren't there on the closed track and only imaginary.

There could be other cars nearby the AI self-driving car, though they might be virtual cars. The AI doesn't realize these cars aren't there and assumes they are real cars. There could be trucks, buses, trains, and so on. You might even have animals such as a dog chasing a cat onto the street.

This is harder to pull-off than it might seem at first glance. If you only had static virtual elements that stood in place, it might be somewhat easier to do this. We would likely though want the virtual cars to be driving next to the actual AI self-driving car and be moving at the same speed as the AI self-driving car. Or, maybe driving behind the self-driving car, then pulling alongside, then passing it, and maybe getting in front of the AI self-driving car and slamming on its brakes.

Can you imagine if we had a human driver do the same thing on the test track? We'd need a stunt driver that would be ready in case the AI self-driving car was unable to brake in time and rammed into the stunt driver's car. Also, how many times could you get the stunt driver to do this same test? Each time would require a restart of the test and you'd be putting that same stunt driver into risk after risk.

As I say, it is certainly advantageous to use this AR approach, but it is also quite tricky to do. You need to intercept the images and video, feed it to the AR system, it needs to figure out what virtual elements are to be included and what movement they should have, and it then needs to feed the overlaid images and video into the AI self-driving car.

The AR needs to know the GPS positioning of the AI self-driving car and its movement so that the AR can properly render the faked virtual elements. This is a computationally intensive task to figure out the AR elements and especially if we add lots of virtual elements into the scene. There might be a dozen faked pedestrians, all at different parts of the scene. We might have a dozen faked cars that are driving nearby the AI self-driving car, alongside it, behind it, in front of it, and so on. Keeping track of the virtual world and making sure it moves with the moving of the AI self-driving car is a challenging computational task.

We likely would also want to feed the responses of the AI that are being used in issuing the car controls commands for the self-driving car to also be fed into the AR. This would allow the AR to gauge what the AI is likely perceiving and thus allow the AR to adjust the virtual world appropriately.

All of this electronic communication and computational effort must be done in real-time and match to the real-world that the AI is supposed to be facing. Latency is a huge factor in ensuring this works as desired for testing purposes.

Here's what I mean. Suppose the AI normally gets the images and video fed to it every millisecond (just a made-up example). The AR is intercepting the images and video before it reaches the AI. Let's assume the AR is running on a computer off-board of the AI self-driving car and so we need to push the images and video via electronic communication to that off-board location. There's time involved in that transmission.

The AR then needs to take time to computationally decide where to place the next round of virtual elements. Once it renders those elements, it now needs to transmit then back over to the AI self-driving car. We've just used up time to electronically communicate back-and-forth with the AI self-driving car. We also used up time to figure out and render the virtual world elements into the images and video.

Suppose it took an extra millisecond or two to do so. The AI self-driving car now is getting data delayed from the sensors by that one millisecond or more. It could be that the AI self-driving car, moving along at say 90 feet per second, might now have less time and less chance to do something that it otherwise could have done in a real-world setting that was absent of the AR. We might have inadvertently pinched the AI by adding the AR into the sequence of actions and now the AI is no longer going to be able to react as it could if the AR was not there at all.

Instead, we've got to get the AR virtual world aspects to be seamless and not at all disruptive to the normal operation by the AI of the self-driving car. I'll add more to the complexity by pointing out that the AR is likely also going to want to be receiving other information from the test track infrastructure. We might for example have other real cars on the test track, perhaps being driven by humans, and so that needs to be taken into account too while the AR does its computations.

We're talking about a sophisticated looping structure that must be buttoned down to be timely and not interfere with the AI of the self-driving car.

If we have several AI self-driving cars being tested at the same time, each of them needs their own rendering of the virtual world elements as specific to where those self-driving cars and what they are doing.

At the University of Michigan's Mcity test track, they are making strides toward this kind of AR and real-world testing. In a recent paper entitled "Real World Meets Virtual World: Augmented Reality Makes Driverless Vehicle Testing Faster, Safer, and Cheaper," researchers Henry Liu and Yheng Feng describe two fascinating examples that they have undertaken with this approach.

The first example involves the use of a virtual train.

Suppose you wanted to determine whether an AI self-driving car will let a moving train pass bye before the AI opts to continue the self-driving car on a path forward. At a test track, you could maybe be lucky enough to have train tracks. You might arrange to rent a train and the train conductor. Maybe you get the train to go back-and-forth on the test track and you run the AI through this drill several times. Let's also hope that the AI self-driving car does not make a mistake and become smushed into a little ball by a train that rams it because the AI misjudged and put the self-driving car onto the tracks in front of the oncoming train. Ouch!

By using AR, the researchers were able to have a computer-generated freight train that appeared to the AI self-driving car as though it was an actual train. To make matters more interesting, they included three virtual cars that were ahead of the real-world AI self-driving car. This is the handy aspect of the AR approach. You can readily switch the scenario and add and subtract elements, doing so without the usual physical and logistical nightmares involved in doing so.

Their second example involved doing a classic "running a red light" as a test of whether the AI self-driving car could sufficiently detect that a wayward car was going to run a red light and take appropriate evasive action by the AI self-driving car.

This also provided a less costly and safer means of doing this kind of test. The fatalities rate for colliding with a red light runner are relatively high in comparison to other kinds of collisions, and thus being able to test to see that the AI can handle a red light running situation are prudent.

How many millions of miles might a public road testing need to occur before an AI self-driving car might perchance encounter a red light runner that happened to also threaten the path of the AI self-driving car?

Well, come to think of it, where I live, it happens much too often, but anyway I assume you get my drift.

Conclusion

Using AR for closed track testing can be a significant boon to overcoming the usual concerns that a closed track does not provide a sufficient variety of scenarios and that it can be overly costly and logistically arduous to setup for a multitude of scenarios.

One aspect about the AR testing is whether to include only the visual aspects of the AR, which is what we as humans are used to too, or whether to also include the other sensory devices as part of the mix of what the AR is essentially spoofing.

An AI self-driving car typically has a multitude of sensors, including cameras, radar, sonar, ultrasonic, and LIDAR.

The sensor fusion portion of the system combines these together to get a more robust indication of what surrounds the AI self-driving car. If one sensor is not functioning well, perhaps obscured by dirt on the camera lenses or maybe it is nighttime, the sensor fusion often has to consider the other sensory inputs with a greater weight.

If the AR does only the visual sensory augmentation, it means that the other sensors aren't going to be able to play a part in the testing.

This is less than ideal since the real-world public roadways will involve presumably all of the sensors and a delicate balance of relying on one or the other, depending upon the situation at hand.

You also need to make sure that the AR virtual elements act and react as they would in the real-world.

Pedestrians do wacky things.

Bicyclists dare cars all the time.

Other car drivers can be wild and swerve into your lane.

It is crucial that the virtual elements be setup and programmed to act in a manner akin to the real-world.

There is still plenty of room to mature the AR capabilities for the testing of AI self-driving car in closed track settings. I guess if we want to attract younger engineers to also aid in making progress, perhaps we might need to include Pikachu, Charizard, Mewtwo, Misty, and Mew into the AR overlays for the test track. We certainly don't want any AI self-driving cars running down a Pokémon.

That's an accident we surely want to avoid.

.

CHAPTER 6

SLEEPING INSIDE
AN
AI SELF-DRIVING CAR

CHAPTER 6

SLEEPING INSIDE

AN

AI SELF-DRIVING CAR

When I was working on my doctorate some years ago, doing so at a prominent west coast university, I decided that during the summer break I would go visit various doctoral colleagues that were doing their PhD's at east coast universities, along with meeting faculty at those institutions as a form of introduction about my research and efforts.

I was going to fly to the east coast on the cheapest flight I could find and would have to pinch pennies during the multi-week adventure. I would be using a compact rental car to drive to campuses such as MIT, Harvard, BU, Yale, Princeton, etc. and it would be my largest overall expense for the trip.

I was a starving student at the time and was trying to stay within a minimal budget for the trip.

Once I arrived to the east coast and had picked-up the rental car, I drove to the first of the series of campus visits. I had not booked any hotels as yet and figured that once I got to a particular university, I'd find a nearby inexpensive hotel to stay the night and then continue onward to the next campus. Upon trying to find a hotel that first night, I discovered that the only rooms available were quite highly priced and it seemed a shame to pay such an exorbitant cost for just a place to sleep for the night.

I decided therefore to sleep in the rental car for the night.

Sounds kind of questionable, I realize.

I was not destitute. It just seemed like the easiest way to do things at the time. No need to check-in and check-out and I would avoid the hotel cost. When I had walked around the campus and met with some of the doctoral students, they showed me the campus gym and explained that anyone could make use of it, though this was not publicized per se. In essence, even a non-student of the campus could use the gym. I decided that since I was going to sleep in my car, I could use the campus gym the next morning to get a shower and shave and be tidied-up accordingly and be prepared for visiting the next campus on my list.

Overall, this is the same approach I used for the entire trip. I would drive to the next campus on my list, stay the day and make visits with various contacts, sleep the night in my rental car, get up and use the campus gym, and then proceed onward to the next destination. I actually somewhat enjoyed the adventure of it. Besides avoiding the cost of the hotels, it was logistically a lot easier to simply find a place to park the car and get some shut-eye.

I did learn some handy lessons about sleeping in a car.

First, I slept in the backseat since the front seats were separate bucket seats and it would not be possible to sleep across the two seats. When I tried to recline the drivers seat all the way back to see if I could sleep in that position, it would not go far enough back to let me lay relatively prone. If I slept in the front row drivers seat it would be like sleeping in a seat on a plane. I opted instead to sleep in the backseat since I could lay down. Unfortunately, I was too tall and could not completely stretch out, but this was not too bad and if I merely curled-up I was able to passably sleep on the backseat.

For the first night, I had parked on-campus in a parking lot that was near to the research building that I visited my fellow doctoral students. I did not realize that there was a rule that no overnight parking was allowed in that parking lot. Sure enough, at about 3 a.m., a campus security guard tried to put a ticket on my windshield. In so doing, he noticed that there was a human actually in the car (that was me!) and rapped on the car window to awaken me. I groggily rolled down the window and he explained that I could not stay parked there. I apologized and woke-up sufficiently to go find a different place to park my rental car and then continue my snooze.

I was wearing my jacket as I slept in the rental car at night, but eventually I realized that I was stinking up my jacket by my evening sleeping and it would have to last me during the daylight hours too. I went and purchased an inexpensive blanket so that I could use it over me when I was sleeping in the car. I selected a blanket that was non-descript and the colors matched the interior of the car. I thought this would be a means to disguise my sleeping in the backseat. Anyone that looked into the window of the car would only see a bland looking blanket that happened to be somewhat bulky looking, which was due to the fact that it had me underneath it.

Part of the reason too that I wanted to be covered while sleeping in the backseat was due to the aspect that people tended to look into the car during the late evening and early morning hours.

I never realized that people would be nosy enough to glance into cars, but they do. I was surprised on the first few nights to have quite a number of walking passerby's that looked into the car. Keep in mind that I was relatively well hidden at this point and so it wasn't as though they had somehow caught a glimpse of a person inside the car and thus naturally would have gotten their curiosity going. I was tempted to put up makeshift window shades to give me some greater privacy, though it seemed a bit extreme and also I assumed it might actually draw undue attention to the car.

I learned the hard way that light and sound can be a significant factor in sleeping. When I got to the third campus of my journey, I parked in the morning in a parking lot that seemed to allow for overnight parking. What I failed to notice was that I had parked directly under a street light that was setup in the parking lot. In fact, this parking lot happened to have some of the brightest night time lighting I had ever seen. When I settled into the car for my night's sleep, I tried to pull the blanket entirely over my head and hoped that the light would not impact my sleep. It kept me up for most of the night.

Speaking of light, there's nothing like the morning sunrise to also potentially wake you up. Most of the trip, I tended to get up once the sun had risen. This was partially due to the light that shined inside the car, and also due the aspect that the car would start to get rather warm inside as the sun beat down on the exterior of the car. The heating of the interior and the light were enough to wake me up, and I dare say probably wake-up most people.

In terms of sounds, I am a relatively light sleeper and have a tendency to wake-up if there are strong sounds or unusual sounds. I was sleeping even more lightly too due to sleeping inside a car. I dreaded the possibility that vandals might try to break into my car, doing so while I was sleeping in it. Or, suppose a car thief opted to try and break-in and steal the car. Imagine me on national TV, waving frantically while in the back-seat, essentially being car-jacked, though the thief might have only been seeking to steal the rental car and did not realize a human was in the backseat.

Anyway, the sounds of people walking past the car were usually not enough to awaken me. But, on several occasions, having parked mainly on college campuses, there would be those drunken undergrads (well, Okay, I realize they might have been grad students too) wandering around and yelling and screaming and having a good old time. This woke me up. One time a street sweeper came up to my car and swept around it. The sounds woke me up. Generally, there were a wide variety of sounds and most of the time it would stir me to wake-up.

In case you are wondering whether I unduly weathered the interior of the rental car, I assure you that when I turned-in the rental car it was no worse for the wear due to my sleeping in it. You would not have had any means of knowing that I had slept in the car. The best news was that I saved literally several thousand dollars by avoiding the nightly costs of being in a hotel over those many weeks of my trip.

Also, I only sleep about 6 hours a night anyway and so mainly did things at the campuses until late in the evening, got into my "sleeper" usually past midnight, and was up and going once the sun rose. Why use a hotel for such a short stint, was my thinking at the time. Furthermore, the college campuses had all the other resources I needed. I was able to work out, shower, change clothes, wash clothes, and do other such chores at the campuses.

It was quite a memorable several weeks and I realize now that sleeping in my car seems a bit off-putting to most people when I tell the story of it. I didn't tell anyone at the time that I was doing so and knew that if I did they would think it was quite peculiar. In my mind, I didn't see any difference between renting an RV and using it to drive around and then use it for sleeping at night and doing the same thing with a conventional car. Sure, the conventional car is not quite as accommodating, but the idea is the same. The notion was to use the vehicle that got you from place to place as the means to also sleep in it. That seemed logical to me. Would you look askance at someone that rented an RV for a several weeks trip? I think not.

As an aside, I had read once that humans supposedly have evolved in a manner such that we prefer to sleep in a cool and dark location, one that is relatively noiseless, something akin to a cave. This makes sense since it would be best to be in a protected place to be somewhat safe from predators and also mitigate the outdoors environmental conditions while you are sleeping. My rental car was my cave. It just so happened that I was a mobile cave, in the sense that I was able to take my cave with me.

Several years after my starving student trip, I came to realize that sleeping inside a car can have nearly magical properties. Here's the skinny on that.

When my children were first born, they sometimes at night would have a hard time sleeping. As anyone with newborns knows, babies can have the worst sleeping cycles. You might find yourself never getting much sleep during the night as they awaken frequently and unexpectedly. It could be they have some gas in their stomach and need to burp it out. It could be they have a full diaper that needs changing. It could be that they just aren't sleepy anymore. It could be a thousand different reasons.

After several nights of being continually disrupted in trying to sleep when they were sleeping, I had a thought that prompted me to try something. Whenever I had driven the kids to see the doctor or over to go shopping, they tended to fall asleep in their baby seats in the car. I would have to awaken then when we reached our destination. It was nearly a sure fire way to presumably get them to fall asleep.

I decided to give this a try late one night when they were fusing and would not go to sleep. I drove around the neighborhood with them safely tucked away in their baby seats. Sure enough, they fell asleep. It was a miracle! I assumed it was either the motion of the car that soothed them, or perhaps it was the feeling of being snugly packed into their car seat, or some other such reason. I didn't really care why it worked, it just plain worked and that was good enough.

Once they seemed fully immersed in sleep, I would drive back to the house and gingerly move them into the house. If I did anything jarring or made any sudden moves, they would awaken right away. Most of the time, by treading very carefully, I was able to use the short car drive to get them into a sleeping state, and then transfer them into the house and they would remain asleep for quite some time. This was obviously better than trying to give them some kind of prescribed or over-the-counter medication to get them to sleep.

This method was by far more effective than rocking their baby sleeper by hand or putting them into one of those automatic rocking baby carriages. The car seemed to have magical powers. It could get them into a sleeping mode that was assured. The funny thing is that to this day, now they are much older, and they report that they do sometimes find themselves starting to fall asleep when a passenger in a car at nighttime. Did I create a habit that now will be with them forever? Or, was I merely tapping into a natural born instinct? Another one of life's mysteries of nature versus nurture.

I don't want you to though assume that there weren't some potential downsides to the nighttime sleeping drives. There was some occasions that they would fall victim to motion sickness. I felt bad about that. It would seem to make their tummies go sour and they might spit-up because of it. Luckily, this was relatively rare. There are some people that are quite prone to motion sickness while inside a moving car. They seemed to not succumb to this and it was rare that they exhibited any car motion sickness symptoms.

What does this have to do with AI self-driving cars?

At the Cybernetic AI Self-Driving Car Institute, we are developing AI software for self-driving cars. One aspect that can be expected to occur would be that people will likely want to sleep in their AI self-driving cars, doing so from time-to-time. As such, the AI ought to be established to appropriately deal with sleeping human occupants.

Allow me to elaborate.

I'd like to first clarify and introduce the notion that there are varying levels of AI self-driving cars. The topmost level is considered Level 5. A Level 5 self-driving car is one that is being driven by the AI and there is no human driver involved. For the design of Level 5 self-driving cars, the auto makers are even removing the gas pedal, brake pedal, and steering wheel, since those are contraptions used by human drivers. The Level 5 self-driving car is not being driven by a human and nor is there an expectation that a human driver will be present in the self-driving car. It's all on the shoulders of the AI to drive the car.

For self-driving cars less than a Level 5, there must be a human driver present in the car. The human driver is currently considered the responsible party for the acts of the car. The AI and the human driver are co-sharing the driving task. In spite of this co-sharing, the human is supposed to remain fully immersed into the driving task and be ready at all times to perform the driving task. I've repeatedly warned about the dangers of this co-sharing arrangement and predicted it will produce many untoward results.

Let's focus herein on the true Level 5 self-driving car. Much of the comments apply to the less than Level 5 self-driving cars too, but the fully autonomous AI self-driving car will receive the most attention in this discussion.

Here's the usual steps involved in the AI driving task:
- Sensor data collection and interpretation
- Sensor fusion
- Virtual world model updating
- AI action planning
- Car controls command issuance

Another key aspect of AI self-driving cars is that they will be driving on our roadways in the midst of human driven cars too. There are some pundits of AI self-driving cars that continually refer to a utopian world in which there are only AI self-driving cars on the public roads. Currently there are about 250+ million conventional cars in the United States alone, and those cars are not going to magically disappear or become true Level 5 AI self-driving cars overnight.

Indeed, the use of human driven cars will last for many years, likely many decades, and the advent of AI self-driving cars will occur while there are still human driven cars on the roads. This is a crucial point since this means that the AI of self-driving cars needs to be able to contend with not just other AI self-driving cars, but also contend with human driven cars. It is easy to envision a simplistic and rather unrealistic world in which all AI self-driving cars are politely interacting with each other and being civil about roadway interactions. That's not what is going to be happening for the foreseeable future. AI self-driving cars and human driven cars will need to be able to cope with each other.

Returning to the topic of sleeping inside an AI self-driving car, let's consider some of the ramifications about doing so and how the AI should be designed and developed to accommodate this likely aspect.

Let's start by dividing up the matter into two parts, there is the situation of sleeping while in a moving car, and a separate matter involves sleeping in a parked car.

My story about having visited numerous college campuses and sleeping in my car overnight is an example of sleeping in a parked car. I had mentioned several lessons learned from that experience.

An AI self-driving car should presumably be a "partner" in assisting any human occupants that might want to sleep inside the AI self-driving car when it is parked. This consists of the AI offering to find a suitable place to park the AI self-driving car.

I realize that some pundits would say that it is not up to the AI to help determine where to park the self-driving car and that instead this is a matter entirely for the human occupants to decide. I'd vote instead that it be a two-way street, of sorts, in that the human occupants might offer ideas or suggestions of where to park the self-driving car, of which the AI might try and ascertain the suitability. Likewise, the AI might offer suggestions and see what the human occupants think of the proposed locations. This would be an interactive NLP (Natural Language Processing) dialogue between the human occupants and the AI.

The AI might have a sophisticated GPS and mapping system access that could let it know whether the place to park is appropriate. Perhaps it is illegal to park where the human occupants want to sleep inside the car. Maybe it's a location that is rampant with crime and thus might be considered riskier to park there for sleeping purposes. And so on.

In fact, there are some that predict that in the future, since AI self-driving cars will be prevalent, and since people will be using their AI self-driving cars 24x7, we might have special parking areas for those that want to indeed sleep inside their AI self-driving car. The AI system might have access to a database indicating those locations. Perhaps it might even use a blockchain for purposes of booking and paying to be able to park there.

Please realize that the future might be quite different than things are today. I mention this because it might become relatively commonplace to sleep inside your parked AI self-driving car. In my case of sleeping in a rental car for my campuses journey, it seemed likely odd to you. It is predicted that due to the ridesharing economy that will be spurred by the advent of AI self-driving cars, sleeping inside an AI self-driving car will be considered ordinary and routine.

Why will things be different about sleeping in a car? First, you will be able to presumably go greater distances by having an AI automated system that can drive your car for you. Rather than taking a train that perhaps has a sleeper compartment, you might instead just get into your AI self-driving car and tell it to drive you from say Los Angeles to Chicago. You'll likely sleep inside the AI self-driving car during that lengthy trip.

Also, the interior of AI self-driving cars is going to likely be different than the interior of today's conventional cars. If you remove the driver controls such as the steering wheel and the pedals, you no longer need to have a driver's seat that is fixed into position at the front of the car.

Instead, most designs suggest that we'll have swivel seats in AI self-driving cars, allowing the human occupants to swivel around and see each other directly and chat with each other. No more of the backseat facing the backs of the front seat passengers.

It is also envisioned that the swivel seats might be convertible into being sleeper seats. They either will recline to allow for sleeping, or maybe connect with each other to make a bed, or perhaps be removable and you can readily place inside a sleeper "seat" when you know in-advance that you are going to be sleeping during a driving trip.

For some people it is hard to imagine a future in which we all will be willingly and purposely wanting to sleep in our cars. Today, you usually only hear about sleeping in a car when it is someone that is homeless and has no other choice of a place to sleep. In fact, here in Los Angeles, there is an ongoing heated debate about sleeping in cars. Where should someone be allowed to sleep in their car? Do they need to move the car every so often or can they park it in-place and leave it there? Does sleeping in cars potentially raise health concerns and other societal considerations? And so on.

As a society, we are likely to go from perceiving sleeping in a car as something untoward to instead it will become a norm of a kind. When I say this, please note that there is a difference between "living" in your car and sleeping from time-to-time in your car. If you park a car at a spot and leave it there for months at a time and sleep and live out of it, this seems different than using an AI self-driving car that generally is going to be in-motion and from time-to-time will need to park someplace. The parking would also likely include recharging the car, assuming that it is an Electrical Vehicle (EV), along with letting the human occupants sleep too.

Overall, one would expect that an AI self-driving car will nearly always be in-motion rather than sitting someplace for someone to sleep in it. The cost of the AI self-driving car is likely to be affordable by being offset by the money that can be made by using it as a ridesharing service. One would assume that the human occupants will pay mainly for the time that the AI self-driving car is taking them to their desired destination. When the AI self-driving car is parked, it is less likely to be making money.

Of course, there are some ridesharing arrangements that will likely include the ability to pay for sleeping while the AI self-driving car is parked. It's another way to make some bucks.

One potential danger about parking an AI self-driving car just anyplace might be the potential for robojacking. Robojacking involves someone trying to steal your AI self-driving car, and you are inside of it when they do so.

Remember how I had mentioned that when I was parking on college campuses that I dreaded the possibility of a car thief trying to steal my car when I was "hiding" inside on the backseat while sleeping? The same worry could occur with AI self-driving cars.

Some would argue that it makes little sense for a car thief to merely steal the AI self-driving car itself, because presumably the only humans allowed to give commands to the AI would be those properly registered to do so. Therefore, the car thieves will be incentivized to only steal the AI self-driving car when there is a human occupant in it, and presumably they can pressure the human occupant to instruct the AI self-driving car for them in their heinous crime. That's an adverse consequence, for sure.

I'd like to next consider the aspects of sleeping as it relates to being in a moving AI self-driving car.

Recall that I told the story of using my conventional car to take my young children for late night short drives to get them to fall asleep. That's an example of a car being in-motion and sleeping in it. With the advent of true Level 5 AI self-driving cars, no longer will we have a human driver that might inadvertently fall asleep at the wheel. There isn't a human driver involved at all. Instead, any of the human occupants being chauffeured by the AI can opt to fall asleep whenever they darned well please to do so.

One prediction is that people might choose to live much further from work than they do today. The logic is that they can merely get into their AI self-driving car and tell it to take them to work. They can even catch some extra winks during the commute. Here in Los Angeles, it is rather ordinary to have a commute time of one to two hours for driving to work. I realize you might urge us to use mass transit, but that's not really taken ahold and instead people continue to drive their cars.

Your commute of one to two hours might consist of you sleeping inside your AI self-driving car while it drives you to work or brings you home after a workday. You might also decide to live further away from work, maybe living further away allows you to get a larger piece of property and at a cheaper price than living closer to work. The nice thing is you don't need to worry about the driving, since it will be done for you by the AI. Plus, you can sleep while it is doing the driving.

Let's consider this notion of sleeping while the AI is driving the self-driving car.

First, you'd need to be rather trusting to be willing to fall asleep while the AI is driving the self-driving car. I would argue that your trust is presumably already going to be high if you are even allowing the AI to drive the self-driving car when you are awake. In other words, if you are awake and it is driving, there is not much you are going to be doing about the driving task anyway. You aren't expected to intervene in the driving for a Level 5 self-driving car. You are along for the ride.

If it is the case that while awake you are doing little about the driving, it would seem that you've already placed your trust into the abilities of the AI to drive the self-driving car. The step of then falling asleep does not seem like much of a logical leap. I realize it is still a bit chilling perhaps to be asleep and completely vulnerable, while if you are awake that at least you might be able to see that accident about to happen, but anyway, in theory, we will all gradually become accustomed to binge able to sleep while inside an in-motion AI self-driving car.

Here's where the AI then comes to play in a manner more so than when the self-driving car is parked. Let me explain.

Suppose you have fallen asleep while the AI self-driving car is heading to your work. Maybe there is a snarl on the freeway and so the AI decides to take a different route, going to side streets. Normally, let's assume that the AI would have let you know that the freeway is crowded, and it is intending to take an alternative route. If you were awake, you might carry on a dialogue with the AI via its NLP and either agree to the rerouting or insist to remain on the freeway. You might have good reasons to not go to the side streets.

Should the AI wake you up to let you know that it is desirous of rerouting the self-driving car? This seems like a rather simple question, I realize.

I am betting that some AI developers though have their own beliefs on this. Some AI developers would say that there is no need to awaken the human occupant and that the AI should just proceed as it deems necessary. If the human has chosen to fall asleep, they will have defacto given full control over to the AI. Meanwhile, there are some other AI developers that would contrarily insist that of course the AI should awaken the human occupants. It is the polite and proper thing to do. The AI needs to make sure that the human occupants are aware of what the AI is doing and that they have willingly and openly agreed to whatever the driving task is that is being performed by the AI.

There you have it, the usual on-and-off world or bits-and-bytes or 0-or-1 binary perspective that many computer-focused people have. It would be unlikely that those with such a mindset might consider to ask the human occupants *beforehand* what they want to have happen once they fall asleep.

This would require too that the AI anticipate the sleeping aspect and be "programmed" accordingly. I'm sure that some would say that's version 2.0, once enough people get upset that their AI either didn't awaken them when it should have, or the AI did waken them and they are upset that it did so.

Speaking of waking up, the AI could serve as a kind of alarm clock too. You might not want to sleep the entire time during your commute to the office, and instead want a few minutes of waking up time before the AI self-driving car reaches the office. In that case, you might tell the AI to awaken you before arriving at the office. You might even indicate that the AI should swing through a Starbucks just as it is going to be waking you, allowing you to drink some coffee as a means to further awaken before reaching work.

This brings up another aspect about the AI and sleeping human occupants. Should the AI be clever enough to know who is asleep in the self-driving car?

Suppose you are in the AI self-driving car and have another adult with you and a child. The child falls asleep during the driving journey. The AI could potentially detect that the child has fallen asleep.

This might seem creepy, but keep in mind that it is likely that most AI self-driving cars will have cameras pointing to the interior of the self-driving car. For those that will be renting out their AI self-driving car for ridesharing purposes, they are bound to want to keep track of what people are doing inside of their self-driving car. You might say that if the ridesharing was being done by a human driver, the human driver would presumably be doing the same kind of watching and would likely realize when someone has fallen asleep in the car.

I would suggest that it will be feasible for the AI to potentially detect when someone is asleep inside the self-driving car. If it does have that kind of functionality, what would it do? One aspect might be to try and create an interior environment that is conducive to sleeping. This might include dimming any interior lighting, it might involve drawing down shades on the car windows, it might include turning off any music or making it quieter, it might involve adjusting the interior temperature, etc.

There is also the motion sickness aspect to be dealt with. If people are going to be routinely sleeping in their in-motion AI self-driving cars, our society is likely going to be experiencing a lot more motion sickness overall (due to the sheer volume of people henceforth sleeping in moving cars). The AI could try to minimize the chances of motion sickness. This might also include trying to keep the self-driving car from taking tight and fast turns or doing any kind of car jerking motions that would otherwise normally arise while driving the self-driving car.

When I say the word "sleeping" you might be thinking of long sleep periods such as several hours of being asleep. That's one way to sleep inside a self-driving car. You might also want to take so-called cat naps. Perhaps you are tired from your last appointment as a salesperson that uses your self-driving car to go from client to client. You want just a few minutes of rest before you get to your next client. You might tell the AI that you are going to shut your eyes and it should wake you up in about 10 minutes.

This brings up another facet of the AI and human occupant interactions. I mentioned earlier that the AI might be able to detect whether there are human occupants sleeping. Another aspect would be for the human occupant to tell the AI that they are intending to go to sleep. Hey, AI, you might say, I want to sleep for the next 20 minutes. You might also add that if anything unusual occurs, it should wake you up and not let you continue sleeping.

There are some that suggest we might even have the AI try to help lull you into sleep. The AI might automatically go into the "sleeping human" mode and try to dim the lighting and modify the temperature and so on. Plus, it could perhaps play soothing music that is intended to help you get to sleep. Some might even say that the AI will be good enough that it could talk you into sleep, almost like a therapist might be able to do so. I admit that I did sometimes recite Dr. Seuss to my kids to get them to sleep inside the car, for which they were too young to understand the words, but I believe that the calm voice and reassuring tones helped them to get to sleep.

Suppose a human awakens and they are so groggy that they try to get out of the self-driving car, not realizing they are inside a moving self-driving car? Or, maybe the human is the kind of person that is prone to sleepwalking. They might unbuckle their seat belt and try to get out of the car, yet still be completely asleep. These kinds of "edge" cases or corner cases will need to be dealt with by the AI.

It could be that the AI might do some kind of wakefulness "test" to ensure that the human is fully awake and aware of their surroundings. Maybe the AI keeps the doors locked while the AI self-driving car is in motion and won't unlock them, though this is somewhat 1984-like and we'll need to decide as a society if that's what we want to happen.

Suppose you put your small child into the AI self-driving car and do so to have the AI drive the child to pre-school. You aren't going to travel with the child. There is no adult in the self-driving car. The child falls asleep on the way to the pre-school. The AI self-driving car arrives at the pre-school. The child is still asleep. What then?

The AI might have an alarm clock mode, as mentioned earlier. This could be activated on a timer basis or might be activated upon arrival at the destination. I know that some people are heavy sleepers and it takes quite a bit to awaken them. A former roommate was notorious for refusing to wake-up, even though he had an alarm clock that sounded as loud as Big Ben. I nearly built a contraption that would pour a bucket of water on his head if he did not awaken when the alarm clock sounded.

In any case, the AI could try speaking at the child to awaken them, hey kid, wake-up. Or, it could honk the horn, which you would think might be sufficient to wake someone up, though admittedly a well-built car often deadens exterior noises well enough that even a honking horn is not jarring while inside the car that has the honking horn.

Via Machine Learning (ML), the AI might be able to discern patterns of human behavior regarding the use of the self-driving car.

You tend to sleep in your self-driving car during your morning commute on Monday's and Thursday's, and thus the AI anticipates your like chance of falling asleep during those days and times. You are the type of person that prefers to be awake when driving past an accident scene, and therefore the AI opts to wake-up in such instances, assuming that you are otherwise asleep.

These kinds of patterns can be utilized to create a kind of "deep personalization" for you of the AI of your self-driving car.

Conclusion

For many of us, the notion that we would sleep like a baby while inside an in-motion AI self-driving car seems completely unreal and surreal.

No way, most people might insist. They want to be awake and watch everything that the AI is doing.

I admit I'm currently in that same camp. It is hard to imagine that we'll perhaps one day have AI self-driving cars that we become so enamored of them that we gracefully and without hesitation fall asleep while inside one, doing so while it is driving on the freeway at 80 miles per hour. Hard to imagine!

Well, anyway, that's what is supposed to eventually happen, namely we will sleep inside a moving AI self-driving car like a baby. I hope it does happen. We are working hard to try and make AI that will inspire that kind of confidence and trust.

In fact, I seem to be missing a lot of sleep trying to make this occur, but I suppose that someday I'll be able to catch-up on the lost sleep by merely sleeping in my trusted AI self-driving car. AI, please sooth me to sleep, will you?

CHAPTER 7

PREVALENCE DETECTION

AND

AI SELF-DRIVING CARS

CHAPTER 7
PREVALENCE DETECTION
AND
AI SELF-DRIVING CARS

During my daily commute on the hectic freeways of Southern California (SoCal), there are drivers that seem to believe that if they aggressively tailgate the car ahead of them (dangerously so!), such an effort will somehow make the traffic go faster. I am sure that these hostile drivers would gladly push or shove the car ahead of them as though they were at a child's bumper cars ride at an amusement park, if they could do so legally.

I'm not quite convinced that their riding on the tail of the car ahead of them is really achieving what they hope for. Yes, there are some drivers that upon noticing they are being tailgated will speed-up, but a casual observation suggests it is not as many as perhaps the belligerent drivers assume will do so. There are even some drivers that once they spot a tailgater will actually pump their brakes lightly and tend to slow down, apparently believing that this will warn the other nosy driver to back-away and not be so pushy.

I'd guess that whenever the pushy tailgater gets the "I'll stop you" driver ahead of them, it only makes the pushy driver want to go even faster and get more irked about the traffic. There have indeed been road rage incidents involving a "faster" driver that was upset about a "slower" driver and they decided to pull over to the side of the freeway and go to fisticuffs over the matter. Those kinds of wild west duke-it-out moments are a sight to behold and though it is not to be condoned it does make for some visual entertainment when otherwise stuck in snarled traffic.

Another concern about the pushy driver is that if the car ahead of them seems to be blocking progress, the pushiness spills over into other perilous maneuvers too. I've watched many times as a pushy driver came up to the bumper of another car, seemingly got frustrated that the car ahead wasn't moving faster and decided to then scramble to pass the car by frantically swinging into another lane. I purposely herein use the word "frantically" because the pushy driver often does not look to see if there is any gap or room to make the lane change, and just does the lane change without a care as to how it might impact other drivers.

To make matters worse, when you have two pushy drivers that happen to end-up in the same place in traffic, they are then both wanting to be pushy in their own respective ways. Imagine you have plumbing at home that has a bit of a stoppage in it, and there is this gush of water that comes up to try and get around the stoppage. That's what happens when two or more of the pushy drivers come upon a situation wherein there are other cars lolling along that seem to not be going as fast as the pushy drivers wish.

Once the two or more pushy drivers detect that another of their own species is nearby, they will frequently opt to turn the whole situation into a breast-beating gorilla-like challenge. One pushy driver will try to outdo another pushy driver. This turns any frantic maneuvers into even more alarming acts as they will veer towards other cars and use any tactic to get ahead of the other pushy car.

I've seen such crazed drivers opt to use the emergency lane, illegally, in order to pass the other pushy driver, or swing into the HOV lane, illegally, and otherwise create accident-waiting moments on the freeway.

After my many years of witnessing this kind of aggressive driving behavior, you might assume that I've grown used to it and take it for granted. Though I don't get overly alarmed about these pushy drivers, I still nonetheless have kept my driving edge in terms of detecting them and trying to stay clear of them. In other words, I don't just ignore them and pretend they don't exist, but instead I know about their antics and keep my wits about me to be wary of them. This happens somewhat subliminally, and I don't seem to consciously be thinking about their ploys and have assimilated into my driving style the fact that they exist and how to contend with them.

During a vacation break, I went up to a Northern California town that is relatively laid back in terms of how people drive and they weren't nearly as aggressive as the usual Los Angeles drivers that I encounter on SoCal freeways and even on side streets such as in downtown Los Angeles. It was not immediately apparent to me that the driving style in this northern town was any different from my "norm" of driving in Southern California. It was only after having been in the town for a few days that I began to realize the difference.

There was an interesting phenomenon that overcame me during the first day or two of driving in this rather quiet town.

When I observed a car approaching me, doing so via my rear-view mirror, I would instinctively start to react as though the car was going to be a pushy driver. I did this repeatedly. Yet, by-and-large, the upcoming driver did not try the crazed pushiness dance that I was used to in Los Angeles. I wasn't even aware that I was reacting until a passenger in my car noticed that I was slightly tensing up and moving forward when it wasn't necessary to do so (I was trying to create a gap between me and the assumed pushy driver behind me, a form of defensive maneuver in reaction to a pushy driver).

What was happening to me?

I was experiencing prevalence-induced behavioral change. That's a bit of jargon referring to one of the interesting newer areas of exploration about human judgment and social behaviors.

Something that is prevalence-induced refers to your having gotten used to having a lot of whatever the matter consists of (that's the "prevalence" aspect), and you then assume that this high-frequency is still occurring even when it is no longer the case (that's the "induced" aspect). You then even attempt to assert that the high-frequency is still there, though it no longer is (that's the "behavioral change" aspect).

In my case, I was accustomed to the high-frequency of pushy drivers and so I overlaid that same perspective upon driver's in the small town and yet they weren't being pushy drivers at all. My mental model was so ingrained to be watching for and reacting to pushy drivers that I saw pushy drivers when they weren't any longer there.

I was fooling myself into believing there were pushy drivers, partially because I knew or expected that there must be pushy drivers wherever I am driving. Don't misunderstand this point and assume that I was consciously calculating this aspect per se. I was not particularly aware that I was treating other drivers as though they were pushy drivers, until my passenger jogged me out of my mental fog and made me realize how I was driving. I was driving in the same manner I always drive. The problem though was that the driving situation had changed, but I had not changed my mental model.

There's an old classic line that if you have a hammer the rest of the world looks like a nail. Since I had a mental model of being on alert for pushy drivers, I ascribed pushiness to drivers that didn't deserve it. Let's say that in Los Angeles there were 30% of drivers that were pushy, while in this town it was more like 3%. I was still expecting that 30% of the drivers would be pushy, and I mentally fulfilled this notion by assigning pushiness to their efforts, getting the proportion closer to my imagined 30%, regardless of whether their efforts actually met the traditional definition of being a pushy driver.

A study done by researchers at Harvard University, the University of Virginia, Dartmouth University, and NYU recently unveiled some fascinating experiments involving prevalence-induced behavioral change. Most notable perhaps was their study of blue dots and purple dots. The aspects about the dots seemed to catch the attention of the widespread media and was covered extensively both nationally and internationally.

In brief, they showed human subjects an array of 1,000 colored dots. The colors of the dots varied on a continuum of being very purple to being very blue. Subjects were to identify which dots were purple and which were blue (actually, they were asked to indicate which dots were blue and which were not blue). Let's assume that the coverage of blue and purple dots was around half and half. After numerous trials of this activity, the researchers then decreased the number of blue dots and increased the number of purple dots (keeping the same total number of dots).

Some participants in the study got the now re-proportioned mixture of blue and purple dots (the experimental "treatment" group), while the control group participants got the same half-and-half mixture (these were the "stable prevalence" participants). The control group still identified the same overall proportion as before, which is handy because it suggests they were still performing as they had all along.

Meanwhile, the treatment group began to identify dots as blue that were now purple, doing so roughly to seemingly have the same balance of blue and purple dots as they had already gotten used to. One would not expect that they would do so. You would assume that if they were "objectively" examining the dots, they would have identified correctly the newer proportion and have done so by simply accurately stating which dots were blue and which were purple.

The experimenters decided to explore this further and did additional studies. They tried another version in which the number of blue dots was increased, and the number of purple dots was decreased, thus the opposite approach of the earlier experiment. What happened? Once again, the treatment group tended to overinflate by identifying the more prevalent blue dots as purple dots, arriving at the mixture level of the initial trials. The researchers did other variants of the same study including warning the subjects, but the result still came out roughly the same.

Just in case some might argue that dots are not much of a visually complex matter, they redid the experiment with 800 computer-generated human faces. The faces were varied on a continuum of appearing to be very threatening to being not very threatening. Experiments were done similarly to the dot's procedures. Once again, the subjects tended to showcase that they would be influenced by the prevalence aspects.

Why does this matter? The prevalence-induced behavioral change can lead to problematic human behavior. In my story about driving in the small town, my reacting to non-existent pushiness could have inadvertently led to traffic accidents. I enlarged my notion of pushy drivers to include drivers that were not at all being pushy. I was assigning the color blue to purple dots.

Suppose a radiologist that is used to seeing MRI images that are over-and-over are ones with cancer, and then the radiologist comes upon an image that does not have cancer. The radiologist might ascribe cancer when it is not actually present, due to the prevalence-induced aspects. Not a good thing.

There is a danger that we as humans might act or make decisions that are based not on what is right there in front of us, but instead based on what our mental models lead us to believe is there. This might seem startling because you would assume that the facts are the facts, the blue dots are the blue dots and the purple dots are the purple dots. Of course, human interpretation and human foibles can differently interpret what we see, hear, taste, etc.

What does this have to do with AI self-driving cars?

At the Cybernetic AI Self-Driving Car Institute, we are developing AI software for self-driving cars. One aspect of AI self-driving cars is whether they will be able to do a better job at driving than humans can, and also whether the Machine Learning (ML) aspects of the AI will be subject to traditionally human-based foibles.

Allow me to elaborate.

I'd like to first clarify and introduce the notion that there are varying levels of AI self-driving cars. The topmost level is considered Level 5. A Level 5 self-driving car is one that is being driven by the AI and there is no human driver involved. For the design of Level 5 self-driving cars, the auto makers are even removing the gas pedal, brake pedal, and steering wheel, since those are contraptions used by human drivers. The Level 5 self-driving car is not being driven by a human and nor is there an expectation that a human driver will be present in the self-driving car. It's all on the shoulders of the AI to drive the car.

For self-driving cars less than a Level 5, there must be a human driver present in the car. The human driver is currently considered the responsible party for the acts of the car. The AI and the human driver are co-sharing the driving task. In spite of this co-sharing, the human is supposed to remain fully immersed into the driving task and be ready at all times to perform the driving task. I've repeatedly warned about the dangers of this co-sharing arrangement and predicted it will produce many untoward results.

Let's focus herein on the true Level 5 self-driving car. Much of the comments apply to the less than Level 5 self-driving cars too, but the fully autonomous AI self-driving car will receive the most attention in this discussion.

Here's the usual steps involved in the AI driving task:
- Sensor data collection and interpretation
- Sensor fusion
- Virtual world model updating
- AI action planning
- Car controls command issuance

Another key aspect of AI self-driving cars is that they will be driving on our roadways in the midst of human driven cars too. There are some pundits of AI self-driving cars that continually refer to a utopian world in which there are only AI self-driving cars on the public roads. Currently there are about 250+ million conventional cars in the United States alone, and those cars are not going to magically disappear or become true Level 5 AI self-driving cars overnight.

Indeed, the use of human driven cars will last for many years, likely many decades, and the advent of AI self-driving cars will occur while there are still human driven cars on the roads. This is a crucial point since this means that the AI of self-driving cars needs to be able to contend with not just other AI self-driving cars, but also contend with human driven cars. It is easy to envision a simplistic and rather unrealistic world in which all AI self-driving cars are politely interacting with each other and being civil about roadway interactions. That's not what is going to be happening for the foreseeable future. AI self-driving cars and human driven cars will need to be able to cope with each other.

Returning to the topic of prevalence-induced behavioral change, let's consider how this could come to play in the case of AI self-driving cars.

We'll start by mulling over the nature of Machine Learning (ML) and AI self-driving cars. Machine Learning and especially deep learning using large-scale artificial neural networks are being used to be able to aid the processing of data that is collected by sensors on an AI self-driving car. When an image is captured via cameras on the AI self-driving car, the image is potentially processed by pumping it through a trained neural network.

A neural network might have been trained on the detection of street signs. Via analyzing the data of a street scene, the neural network can possibly determine that a Stop sign is up ahead or ascertain the posted speed limit based on a speed limit sign. Likewise, the neural network or an allied neural network might be have been trained on detecting the presence of pedestrians. By analyzing the street scene image, the neural network could be looking for the shape of the arms, legs, body and other physical facets that suggest a pedestrian is up ahead.

It is generally likely that for the time being these Machine Learning algorithms will be pre-trained and not be unleashed to try and adjust and learn new elements while in-the-field. Besides the tremendous amount of potential computing power that would be needed to learn on-the-fly, there would also be the potential danger that the "learning" might go off-kilter and not learn what we would want the system to learn.

For example, suppose the ML began to mistake fire hydrants as being pedestrians, or, perhaps worse so, it began interpreting pedestrians as being fire hydrants. Without some kind of more formalized checks-and-balances approach, allowing an on-the-fly machine learner on a standalone basis in the context of an AI self-driving car is dicey. More likely would be the collecting of data from AI self-driving cars up into the cloud of the auto maker or tech firm involved in the self-driving car, doing so via OTA (Over-The-Air) electronic communications, and the auto maker or tech firm would then use the data for adding machine learning (doing so across the entire fleet of AI self-driving cars). An updated neural network based on the added machine learning could then be pushed back down into the AI self-driving car via the OTA for use in execution of doing improved image analyses.

Besides trying to analyze aspects such as street signs and the presence of pedestrians, another potential use of the Machine Learning would be to look for patterns in traffic situations.

The better that the AI can be at detecting recognizable and relatively repeatable kinds of traffic patterns, the more that the AI can then be prepared to readily and rapidly deal with those particular idiosyncratic traffic aspects.

If the AI is not versed in traffic patterns, it must try in real-time to cope with how to best act or react. Instead, if the traffic pattern is one that has been previously experienced and codified, along with having identified fruitful means of dealing with the traffic pattern, the AI can more gingerly drive the car and drive in a human-like defensive manner.

Suppose an AI self-driving car is driving in Los Angeles and taking me to my office each day. Over and over it collects traffic data indicative of aggressive drivers, which are aplenty here (you can spot them like fish in a barrel). The data gets uploaded to the cloud. An analysis is undertaken and the deep learning adjusts the neural networks, which are then reloaded into my AI self-driving car. Gradually, over weeks or months, the AI self-driving car gets better and better at contending with the pushy drivers.

Here's my question for you – do you think it is possible that the AI might eventually reach a point of anticipating and expecting pushy drivers, so much that it then if taken to a new locale might ascribe the pushiness to non-pushy drivers?

In essence, I am suggesting that the prevalence-induced behavioral change that I had personally experienced, as a human being (which, I declare to you that I am indeed a human being – please rest assured that I am not a robot!), could very well happen to the AI of an AI self-driving car. It is reasonable and conceivable that upon going to that little town up in Northern California, the AI might be watching for aggressive drivers and assume that drivers that aren't pushy are actually indeed pushy, based on the prevalence-induced aspects.

The AI might see blue dots where there are purple dots, if you get my drift.

There are a myriad of other ways in which the prevalence-induced behavioral aspects can arise in the AI of a self-driving car. It will be crucial for AI developers to realize that this kind of human judgement "impairment" can also strike at the underpinnings of the Machine Learning and artificial neural networks used in AI (I'll add that this is true beyond just the topic of self-driving cars, and thus it is something to be considered for any kind of AI system).

How to catch this phenomenon will be a key programming concern for any savvy AI developer that does not want their AI to fall into this prevalence trap.

Besides the AI developers themselves detecting it, which is a human manual kind of check-and-balance, a truly self-aware AI system should have internal system mechanisms to be on the look for this judgement malady.

The AI's self-awareness would be the last line of defense since it would be the portion that while the AI self-driving is in the midst of driving, it would be the prod that would nudge the AI to realize what is afoot. I had mentioned that the passenger in my car was my prod, though I wish it had been my own mind that had noticed it (probably was enjoying being on vacation too much!).

Given that we know that prevalence-induced biases can creep into data and thus into a ML-based system, we need to have some kind of automated anti-prevalence detection and antidote. During my morning commutes, I'll be working on that solutions, along with continuing to keep a watchful eye on those pushy drivers.

CHAPTER 8
SUPER-INTELLIGENT AI
AND
AI SELF-DRIVING CARS

CHAPTER 8

SUPER-INTELLIGENT AI
AND
AI SELF-DRIVING CARS

Paperclips. They quietly do their job for us. Innocent, simple, nondescript. You probably have paperclips right now somewhere near you, doing their duty by holding together a thicket of papers. In the United States alone there are about 11 billion paperclips sold each year. That's about 34 paperclips per American per year. You likely have some straggler paperclips in your pocket, your purse, in the glove box of your car, and in a slew of other places.

Little did you know the danger you face.

There is a paperclips apocalypse heading our way. Locking your doors won't stop it. Tossing out the paperclips you have in-hand won't help. Moving to a remote island will not particularly increase your chances of survival. Face the facts and get ready for the dawning of the paperclips war and the end of mankind.

What am I talking about? Have I gone plain loco?

I'm referring to the everyday-person obscure but also semi-popular in AI "paperclip maximizer" problem. It goes somewhat like this.

As humans, we build some kind of super-intelligent AI. Of the many things we end-up asking the super-intelligent AI to do, one aspect includes that we might request that it make paperclips for us. Seems simple enough. The super-intelligent AI can hopefully do something as relatively easy as running a manufacturing plant to bend little wiry pieces of thin steel and make paperclips for us.

The super-intelligent AI is trying to be as helpful to us as it can be. Almost like a brand-new puppy that will do just about anything to make you happy, including wagging its tail, jumping all over you, and the like, the super-intelligent AI opts to really seriously get into the making of paperclips for mankind. It begins to acquire all of the available steel in the world so as to be able to make more paperclips. It quickly and inescapably opts to convert more and more of our existence and Earth into a magnificent paperclip making factory.

The super-intelligent AI assumes of course that humans will go along with this, since it was humans that started the super-intelligent AI on this quest.

If there are humans that happen to wander along during the quest and try to get in the way of making paperclips, well, those humans will need to one-way-or-another be gotten out of the way. Paperclips must be made. Paperclips are going to flourish and if it takes all of the globe's resources to do so, the super-intelligent AI will find a means to make it occur.

Think of the famous movie *2001: A Space Odyssey* and how HAL, the AI system running the spaceship, tried to stop the astronauts (I'm not going to say much more about the movie because I don't want to spoil the plotline for those of you that haven't seen it, though, come on, you should have already seen the movie!).

This paperclip apocalyptic scenario is credited to Nick Bostrom, an Oxford University philosophy professor that first mentioned it in his now-classic piece published in 2003 entitled "Emotive and Ethical Aspects of Decision Making in Humans and in Artificial Intelligence" (see https://nickbostrom.com/ethics/ai.html) and which eventually became a darling of hypothetical AI super-intelligence takeover discussions and debates.

The paperclips scenario has spawned numerous variants.

I had mentioned herein that we humans asked the super-intelligent AI to make paperclips for us. But, you could also take the position that the super-intelligent AI for whatever reason decided to make paperclips without us humans even asking it to do so.

Notice though that either way, the making of the paperclips seems like a rather innocent and benign act. That's a crucial aspect underlying the nature of the debate. We could of course posit that the super-intelligent AI wants to be overtly evil and is out to kill-off humans, or that it fiendishly plots to make paperclips as a means to destabilize, overthrow, and imprison or destroy all of mankind. This is not the essence though of the paperclip scenario (there are lots of other scenarios that involve that AI as a heinous humanity-destroyer portrayal). Instead, let's go with the theme that the super-intelligent AI happens to get into the paperclip making business and then things go awry.

Let's consider some excerpts of what Bostrom had to say when he first postulated the paperclips scenario.

When discussing the advent of super-intelligent AI -- "It also seems perfectly possible to have a superintelligence whose sole goal is something completely arbitrary, such as to manufacture as many paperclips as possible, and who would resist with all its might any attempt to alter this goal."

And, here's another related excerpt:

"Another way for it to happen is that a well-meaning team of programmers make a big mistake in designing its goal system. This could result, to return to the earlier example, in a superintelligence whose top goal is the manufacturing of paperclips, with the consequence that it starts transforming first all of earth and then increasing portions of space into paperclip manufacturing facilities."

The choice in the scenario of making of paperclips by the imaginary super-intelligent AI was kind of handy since we already accept that paperclips are rather innocent and benign. If the postulation was the making of atomic bombs, it would not have been helpful in the discussion because then we might have all gotten wrapped-up into the fact that what was being made is inherently dangerous and can kill.

In terms of paperclips, though I did one time get a cut from a paperclip, they otherwise are relatively tame and not especially threatening. I have no particular grudge against paperclips and accept them with open arms.

The aspect that the scenario encompasses making paperclips, rather than just admiring them or using them, provides an essential element to the underlying theme. The super-intelligent AI is underway on a task that will require physical materials and the acquisition and consumption of resources. I think we can all envision how this might end-up starving the world by the super-intelligent AI scooping up everything that could be used to make paperclips. A vivid imagery!

For those of you that aren't so keen on the paperclips aspect per se, there are other similar exemplars that are often utilized. For example, you can be a bit more lofty by substituting the role of the paperclips with instead a quest to solve the Riemann Hypothesis.

The Riemann Hypothesis involves a key question about the nature and distribution of prime numbers. Bernhard Riemann proposed a hypothesis about prime numbers in 1859 and mathematicians have been trying to prove or disprove it ever since. It is so important that it is considered a vaunted Millennium Prize Problem and sits in the same ranks as the computer science quest for whether P=NP problem. Some say that true pure mathematicians are continually slaving away at the Riemann Hypothesis and consider it to be one of the greatest unsolved mathematical puzzles.

In the case of the super-intelligent AI, you can scrap the story about the paperclips, and instead replace the paperclips with the super-intelligent AI opting to try and solve the Riemann Hypothesis instead. To solve the mathematical puzzle, the super-intelligent AI once again grabs up the world's resources and uses them to participate in working toward a solution. If humans get in the way of the super-intelligent AI during this quest, those pesky humans will be dispensed with in some fashion or another.

See how that version is a bit more lofty and refined?

Paperclips are mundane. Everybody knows about paperclips. If you juice up the scenario by referring to the Riemann Hypothesis, you'll get others to perceive the scenario as more high-fluting. You can even suggest that ultimately the super-intelligent AI would turn the world into a computronium (there's a word you likely haven't used lately, which indicates that the planet would essentially be turned into one gigantic computing devices, ostensibly used by the super-intelligent AI in this case to try and ferret out the Riemann Hypothesis).

Personally, I usually opt to use the paperclips version since it is easier to explain and also the notion of the super-intelligent AI coopting the world's resources seems to fit better to a situation involving the physical manufacturing of something. Anyway, choose any version that you prefer.

An area of AI known as "instrumental convergence" tends to use the paperclips scenario (or equivalent) as a basis for discussing what might happen once we are able to produce super-intelligent AI systems. The crux is that we might have super-intelligent AI that has the most innocuous of overall goals, such as making paperclips, but for which things go haywire and the super-intelligent AI inadvertently wipes us all out (that's a simplification, but you get the idea).

When I say that things go haywire, I don't want you to infer that the AI has a mistake or fault inside of it. Let's assume for the moment that this super-intelligent AI is working as we designed it and built it to work. Of course, yes, there could be something that goes amiss inside the AI and it goes on a rampage like a crazed Godzilla, but we'll put that to the side for the moment.

Imagine that we've created this super-intelligent AI and it is working as we intended, or at least as far as we were able to look-ahead and be able to imagine what we thought we intended. Keep in mind that maybe we can only see two moves ahead in the game of life, such as a chessboard where we can only see a move or two ahead (often referred to as ply). Perhaps, by the time things get to ply three, we suddenly realize, oops, we goofed up and started something that when it gets to move three it is bad for all of us. Ouch!

Anyway, let's get back to the end-goals matter.

Most of the time, we usually focus solely on the end-goals of these super-intelligent AI systems. Was the end-goal to destroy all of humanity? If so, it certainly makes sense that the super-intelligent AI might do exactly as so built, namely it might attempt to destroy all of mankind and thus succeed at what we set it up to do. Congrats, super-intelligent AI, you succeeded, we're all dead.

The end-goal is almost too easy of a line-of-thought. To go deeper, suppose you have an end-goal that looks pretty good and innocent and satisfactory. Meanwhile, you have intermediary kinds of goals, often not getting as much attention as the end-goals, but nonetheless those intermediary goals are crucial to gradually getting toward the end-goals.

Suppose the intermediary goals inadvertently can allow for the end-goal to get somewhat twisted out-of-shape. This can be by the nature of the intermediary goals themselves and maybe they aren't well stated, or it could be that you omitted an intermediary goal that should have been included.

You might have insufficient intermediary goals that therefore do not provide a proper driver toward the end-goals and thus the attempt to reach the end-goal goes astray accordingly. To make paperclips, I might not have included an intermediary goal that says do not destroy humanity in whatever quest you are undertaking. By omission, I have left vague and available the super-intelligent AI to take actions that achieve the end-goal and yet have rather adverse consequences in doing so.

Some assert that we need to have fundamental AI-drives that will be included in the intermediary goals.

Those fundamental AI-drives are aspects such as the AI having a sense of self-preservation. Another one might be the preservation of mankind. You can liken these AI-drives to something like Issac Asimov's so-called "The Three Laws" which he introduced in his science fiction story in 1942. Be aware that Asimov's Laws are exceedingly simplistic and have been criticized as over-simplifying the foundations for a super-intelligent AI system, which, you also need to keep in mind it was just a science fiction short story and not a design manual for super-intelligent AI of the future.

In any case, the ethical aspects of AI are certainly worthy of attention and this will increasingly be the case.

The more that AI can actually become the futuristic AI that has been envisioned, the closer we get to having to deal with the practical aspects of these various doomsday scenarios. Some are worried that we'll let the horse out of the barn and have come too late to figuring out the AI ethical aspects. It does seem to make sense that we ought to make sure that we iron out these aspects before the super-intelligent AI making paperclips or solving the Riemann Hypothesis destroys us all.

For instrumental convergence, the key takeaway is that we might have relatively decent end-goals for our super-intelligent AI, but the underlying intermediary goals were lacking or omitted that would have led the super-intelligent AI on a more rightful path. The set of so-called instrumental goals or sub-goals, or often referred to as instrumental values, are vital to the journey on the way to the end-goals. An adverse instrumental convergence can occur, meaning that these intermediary goals don't mesh together in a good way and thus fail to stop or prevent distortions during the journey to a seemingly helpful and beneficial end-goal.

This reminds me of when my children were quite young and one day we went to a local park. There were some other children there that we did not know. My children mixed-in with those unfamiliar children, and it was determined by the collective group that they would play a game of capture the flag. This is normally a simple and innocent enough game involving placing an item such as a flag or T-shirt or whatever at one end of the park, doing so for one team, and likewise at the other end for the other team (having then been divided into two teams, or more if they had a lot of kids).

Thus, the end-goal involves capturing the flag of the other team.

Usually, this entails running around and playfully having a good time. The flag capturing was in my view not nearly as crucial as the kids getting some exercise and having a good time. It also involved working together as a group. This was a means to hone their teamwork skills and deal with others that might or might not be familiar with group dynamics. When my kids were very young, there wasn't any group dynamics per se and it was each person just ran wildly. As they got older, working collaboratively with the group became more reasoned.

Well, here's what happened in this one particular instance and it still stands out in my mind because of what took place. Some of the kids opted to pounce on my children and pin them to the ground, incapacitating them so that they could not run and try to help capture the flag. And don't think that this pinning action was delightful or sweet. The bigger kids were pushing, shoving, hitting, kicking, and doing whatever they could to keep my children (and some of the others) pinned to the dirt.

I was shocked. I looked at the other parents that happened to be at the park, and none them seemed to be paying attention and none of them seemed to care about how the game was unfolding. My kids were old enough that they didn't like it when I might try to intervene, and they had reached the age of wanting to take care of themselves. Should I step into this melee? Should I leave it be? I decided to ask one of the parents what they thought of the actions occurring. This particular parent shrugged his shoulders and said that kids will be kids. He was somewhat proud that they had discovered a means to win the game.

The end-goal was to capture the flag. I had assumed that these children would all have somewhat similar intermediary goals such as don't beat-up another kid to win a playful game. That's what my children knew from how I was raising them. Other parents there were obviously raising their children with a different set of instrumental values or instrumental goals, or maybe had omitted some that I had already tried to ingrain in my children.

In any case, this somewhat provides a highlight about what might happen with super-intelligent AI. We could program a super-intelligent AI that has seemingly innocuous end-goals and yet the pursuit of the end-goals could go in a direction that we did not anticipate and nor desire. Whether it is paperclips or solving a mathematical puzzle or capturing the flag, we need to be wary of setting in motion a blind pursuit of an end-goal and for which the utility function that combines together to reach that end-goal has a proper and appropriate balance to it.

You might want to take a look at some of my prior pieces about how AI could become a type of Frankenstein, and also aspects about the AI singularity, and so on.

These "thought experiments" about the future of AI are often seen as somewhat abstract and not especially practical. Is AI going to be an existential threat to humanity? That's quite a way off in the future. There isn't any kind of AI today that even remotely has anything to do with super-intelligence. Debates of this kind will often meander around and cover a lot of ground about the nature of intelligence and the nature of artificial intelligence. Quite interesting and thought provoking, yes, but not especially pertinent to today and nor even likely anytime near-term (nor likely mid-term).

One criticism often tossed around about these debates is that the AI that is supposed to be super-intelligent appears to behave in ways that don't seem to be super-intelligent. Would a truly super-intelligent AI be so super-stupid that it did not realize that the obsession with making paperclips was to the detriment of everything else? What kind of super-intelligent AI is that?

Indeed, in today's world, I'd tend to suggest that super-stupid AI is a much more immediate and worrisome threat than the super-intelligent AI.

When I use the phrase "super-stupid AI" please don't get offended. Is the AI that is running a robotic arm currently in a manufacturing plant and doing some relatively sophisticated work the kind of AI that would be super-intelligent? I'd say no. Is that AI super-stupid? I would say it is closer to being super-stupid than it is being super-intelligent, and thus if you forced me into deciding into which of those two categories it fits into, I'd pick the super-stupid (that's if I was only allowed the two categories).

I would feel safer telling people that come in contact with that AI robotic arm that it is super-stupid, which hopefully would put those people into an alert mode of being cautious around it, versus if I told them it was super-intelligent AI, and for which they might then falsely let down their guard and get clobbered by it. They would likely assume that a super-intelligent AI system would be smart enough to not strike them when they happened to get too close to the equipment.

If you prefer, I can use the phrase super-ignorant instead of super-stupid, which might be more palatable and applicable. But let's for now go with the super-intelligent AI notion that we are going to have super-intelligent AI that also has warts and flaws and acts at times like child that has no comprehension of the world, even though we are calling it super-intelligent. It is a blend of super-stupidity, super-ignorance, and super-intelligence, all mixed into one.

What does this have to do with AI self-driving cars?

At the Cybernetic AI Self-Driving Car Institute, we are developing AI software for self-driving cars. In some ways, the AI being developed and fielded by many of the auto makers and tech firms in the self-driving car realm are akin to the paperclip maximizer problem.

There are AI self-driving cars that are going to have some semblance of super-intelligent AI, combined with super-stupid AI and super-ignorant AI. I'd like to describe how this might occur and also offer indications of what we ought to all be doing because of it.

I'd like to first clarify and introduce the notion that there are varying levels of AI self-driving cars. The topmost level is considered Level 5. A Level 5 self-driving car is one that is being driven by the AI and there is no human driver involved. For the design of Level 5 self-driving cars, the auto makers are even removing the gas pedal, brake pedal, and steering wheel, since those are contraptions used by human drivers. The Level 5 self-driving car is not being driven by a human and nor is there an expectation that a human driver will be present in the self-driving car. It's all on the shoulders of the AI to drive the car.

For self-driving cars less than a Level 5, there must be a human driver present in the car. The human driver is currently considered the responsible party for the acts of the car. The AI and the human driver are co-sharing the driving task. In spite of this co-sharing, the human is supposed to remain fully immersed into the driving task and be ready at all times to perform the driving task. I've repeatedly warned about the dangers of this co-sharing arrangement and predicted it will produce many untoward results.

Let's focus herein on the true Level 5 self-driving car. Much of the comments apply to the less than Level 5 self-driving cars too, but the fully autonomous AI self-driving car will receive the most attention in this discussion.

Here's the usual steps involved in the AI driving task:
- Sensor data collection and interpretation
- Sensor fusion
- Virtual world model updating
- AI action planning
- Car controls command issuance

Another key aspect of AI self-driving cars is that they will be driving on our roadways in the midst of human driven cars too. There are some pundits of AI self-driving cars that continually refer to a utopian world in which there are only AI self-driving cars on the public roads. Currently there are about 250+ million conventional cars in the United States alone, and those cars are not going to magically disappear or become true Level 5 AI self-driving cars overnight.

Indeed, the use of human driven cars will last for many years, likely many decades, and the advent of AI self-driving cars will occur while there are still human driven cars on the roads. This is a crucial point since this means that the AI of self-driving cars needs to be able to contend with not just other AI self-driving cars, but also contend with human driven cars. It is easy to envision a simplistic and rather unrealistic world in which all AI self-driving cars are politely interacting with each other and being civil about roadway interactions. That's not what is going to be happening for the foreseeable future. AI self-driving cars and human driven cars will need to be able to cope with each other.

Returning to the super-intelligent AI, let's consider ways in which AI that is being developed today and fielded into AI self-driving cars is going to be a combination of super-intelligent, super-stupid, and super-ignorant.

I'll start by providing an example that seems rather farfetched, but it was one that I think offers a handy paperclip-like maximizer scenario and is squarely in the AI self-driving car realm.

Ryan Calo, an Associate Professor of Law at the University of Washington in Seattle, offered an intriguing and disturbing circumstance of a fictional AI self-driving car that goes too far in a quest to achieve maximum fuel efficiency and in so doing asphyxiates the human owners of the AI self-driving car:

"The designers of this hybrid vehicle provide it with an objective function of greater fuel efficiency and the leeway to experiment with systems operations, consistent with the rules of the road and passenger expectations. A month or so after deployment, one vehicle determines it performs more efficiently overall if it begins the day with a fully charged battery. Accordingly, the car decides to run the gas engine overnight in the garage, killing everyone in the household" (see his article entitled "Is the Law Ready for Driverless Cars" in the May 2018 issue of the Communications of the ACM, page 34).

This morbid scenario provides another instance of the paperclip maximizer problem.

The AI of the self-driving car was provided with a seemingly innocuous end-goal, namely to achieve high fuel efficiency. Somehow the AI devised an oddball logical contortion that by running the gas engine and depleting the gas it would end-up with a fully charged battery, and it would be able to arrive at the desired end-goal of fuel efficiency. We can quibble about various facets of this scenario and that it has some loose ends (if you dig into the logic of it), but anyway it is another handy example on this matter of super-intelligent AI and how it can get things messed-up.

Let's consider something directly applicable to the emerging AI self-driving cars of today.

Today's AI self-driving cars are going to have Natural Language Processing (NLP) capabilities to converse with the human occupants of AI self-driving cars.

Some falsely think that human occupants will only utter a destination location and then remain silent during the rest of the AI self-driving car driving journey. If you consider this for a moment, you'd realize it is a quite naïve way to consider the needs of the interaction between the AI and the human occupants inside an AI self-driving car. There is likely going to be a need for the human occupant to alter the indicated destination desired and request a different destination, or seek to have intermediary destinations add, or have a concern about the driving aspects, and so on.

Suppose my Level 5 AI self-driving car is parked in my garage and I come out to it since I have a driving trip in mind. I get into the self-driving car and tell the AI that I want to be driven to the grocery store. I lean back in my comfy passenger seat (as a Level 5, there aren't any driver's seats), and await the AI to start the self-driving car and head over to the store. Instead, the AI refuses to start-up the self-driving car.

My first hunch is that the AI is suffering from a fault or failure. I run an internal systems diagnostic test and it reports that the AI is working just fine. I ask the AI again, please, I add to the wording, take me to the grocery store. The engine still doesn't start. The self-driving car remains still. It doesn't look like I'm going to be getting my ride over to the store anytime soon.

Fortunately, this AI happens to have an explanation-generation capability. I ask the AI to explain why my command is not being obeyed. I'd been wondering that maybe I've not phrased my request aptly? Maybe the AI is misunderstanding what I am asking the AI to do? An articulated explanation of the AI's logic for not abiding by my command might reveal where the hold-up seems to be.

The AI reveals that it will not take me to the store because it is not safe to do so. Furthermore, one of its top priority end-goals to always try to make sure that any human passengers in the AI self-driving car are kept safe. Since the end-goal is make sure in this case that I remain safe, and since the AI has ascertained that it is unsafe to drive over to the store, the AI "logically" deduced that it should not take me there and therefore is not going to start on the driving journey.

Impeccable logic, it would seem.

But is this logic absurdity that has gone astray? You could claim that never leaving the garage would always be the safest act of the AI self-driving car. The moment that the AI self-driving car gets onto a roadway and in-motion, the odds of a crash or other incident would certainly seem to rise. To ensure my safety, the AI self-driving car can just sit quietly in the garage and never move. I think we might all agree that this would not be a very useful AI self-driving car if it never left the garage.

This could be an indicator of the paperclip maximizer problem pervading the AI of my AI self-driving car.

I'll add a twist though to showcase that you cannot always jump right away to the paperclips. Suppose that I live in an area that has just been hit by a massive hurricane. The roads are flooded. Electrical power poles have fallen over and there are streets with electrical lines dangling across them. Local emergency agencies have advised the public to stay in place and not venture out onto the roads.

What do you think of the AI now?

It could be that the AI was electronically privy to the hurricane conditions and has determined that the self-driving car should not venture out. My safety is indeed in jeopardy if the AI were to proceed to head to the grocery store. Thank goodness for the AI. Probably saved my life.

Of course, that's not quite the end of the matter, since as a human, perhaps I ought to be able to override the AI hesitation, but that's something I've discussed in several of my other articles and I'll skip covering that aspect herein.

Overall, the paperclips maximizer problem can be quite useful for even today's AI.

It is more than merely an abstract thought experiment about a future world that we might not see for eons to come. You don't necessarily need to have super-intelligent AI to be considering the paperclips threat. Sophisticated AI systems of today that have end-goals and intermediary goals and values can get themselves into a bind by not having a sufficient form of interlacing logic.

I'm especially concerned about AI self-driving cars that are emerging from the auto makers and tech firms and whether or not the AI developers are properly and appropriately worried about the paperclips scenario. They are so focused right now on getting an AI self-driving car to drive on a road and not hit people, which barely scratches the surface of what a true AI self-driving car needs to do, and thus there is not much attention to this kind of "futuristic" paperclips maximizer issue.

Imagine too if the OTA (Over-The-Air) updating capability of an auto maker or tech firm were to send out an updated set of goals and sub-goals that led their entire fleet of AI self-driving cars to get into an unexpected bind. Perhaps all of the AI self-driving cars in their fleet might suddenly come to a halt or take some other untoward action, prompted by conflicting sub-goals and goals, or sub-goals that undermine the end-goals, and so on. I mention this because I've only been discussing herein an individual self-driving car and it's own AI issues, and yet ultimately there will presumably be thousands, hundreds of thousands, or many millions of such cars on our roadways.

Paperclips Apocalypse. Riemann Hypothesis Armageddon. Or, perhaps the AI self-driving car Day-of-Reckoning. Not a rosy picture of the future.

We can already use "thought experiments" to right now figure out that AI self-driving cars need to be designed, programmed, and fielded in a manner that will be beneficial to mankind, and AI developers need to be wise and leery of hidden or unsuspected out-of-control maximizers and other aliments of systems logic that could turn their beloved AI self-driving cars into our worst nightmare.

Either way, I'd advise you to make sure you keep your eye on those paperclips, they might be needed to defuse a super-intelligent AI gone amok.

.

CHAPTER 9
CAR CARAVANS
AND
AI SELF-DRIVING CARS

CHAPTER 9

CAR CARAVANS

AND

AI SELF-DRIVING CARS

I was stuck in traffic the other day when a Presidential motorcade made its way from Los Angeles LAX airport to tony Beverly Hills in sunny Southern California. This caravan of cars included an impressive array of special stretch limos, armored SUV's, and a slew of police vehicles that were making sure that nobody intervened into the VIP line of cars. The police kept ahead of the pact and made sure that intersections were open and ready for the motorcade to flow along without having to stop at any traffic signals.

It caused all of the surrounding or nearby traffic to come to a halt. Some of my colleagues groused at the aspect that we had to wait for the motorcade to pass past us. Why should the motorcade get a higher priority than the rest of us drivers, they bemoaned? I gently tried to point out that waiting a few extra minutes in SoCal traffic is pretty much a daily driving chore anyway, plus it certainly makes sense that to protect those involved in the motorcade it should proceed along quickly. Furthermore, if the motorcade was just part of normal traffic, I pointed out that it probably would inevitably have created even longer waits, especially since the motorcade cars were wanting to stick together as they drove on the roadways.

About a month ago, there was a funeral procession of cars for a famous celebrity, and the procession or caravan of cars started at a funeral home in one location of town and proceeded on a lengthy driving journey to a cemetery in another city where the deceased was to be buried. This was a similar kind of "caravan" as akin to the Presidential motorcade and was guided by police cars to keep the group going along smoothly. In this case, the caravan moved at a much slower pace and the police did not keep all of the intersections open for the entire caravan. Nonetheless, it was another example of a series of cars that were aligned to a joint purpose of trying to drive loosely together.

At self-driving car conferences that I speak at, I've noticed that some people seem to inadvertently confuse the notion of car caravans with the notion of platooning. They are different aspects.

Platooning does include the idea that you have multiple vehicles trying to stay together while driving on a journey, and in that sense, it has apparent similarities to a caravan. With platooning, the goal is to have the cars or trucks be as close together as possible, doing so to potentially optimize fuel savings and reduce pollutant emissions from the vehicles. The vehicles draft off of each other and try to move in very tight unison with each other.

A car caravan usually has a much looser requirement of the caravan participants being so close to each other. Cars can vary their distances from each other, with some at times being close and at other times getting a bit distant of each other. The car caravan does not usually have as a goal the optimization of fuel or the reduction of emissions. Instead, it is more of a symbolic gesture of togetherness that the vehicles all travel together. And, from a traffic perspective, it can be overall more optimal as to reaching their common end-point destination or even intermediary destinations along the way.

The lessons learned about how to best structure and operate a caravan can certainly transfer over to trying to best carryout a platooning operation. Likewise, aspects of doing platooning can be possibly reused when trying to manage a caravan. My main point is that caravans and platooning are not identical, and there are some distinctive differences. I'd say they are of the same species and thus each can glean insights from the other.

Some caravans can be well-prepared in-advance and involve in-depth logistics for planning of the caravan.

I'm sure that the Presidential motorcade had included weeks or months of dialogue with local officials about the path to take through SoCal, along with coordinating with local police, highway patrol, city traffic engineers, etc. There were likely contingencies covered too. I noticed that the motorcade had ambulances and fire trucks that were part of the overall group. I'm assuming that if something had gone amiss while the motorcade was proceeding, those first responders were included as a just-in-case they might be needed right away.

Car caravans can also occur in a somewhat spontaneous fashion and be more ad hoc than formalized.

Allow me to share with you an example of an impromptu kind of car caravan.

I was at a meeting of a professional association that I am a member of, and all of a sudden someone suggested that we all go across town to a popular restaurant and continue our discussions there while catching dinner. Not everyone at the association meeting had driven to the event in their own cars and so we had a somewhat chaotic moment as people offered to give rides to others that also wanted to get to the restaurant. It took a few minutes of a bazaar-like trading effort to figure out who would go in which cars, and whether the cars so chosen could fit that number of people. It was also complicated due to the aspect that once the restaurant dinner was finished, we were trying to solve the secondary problem of whom would get driven home by whom, which added another layer of complexity to the impromptu matter.

Those of us driving were all in agreement as to the destination and the desire to get there in roughly the same amount of time. We all hoped to arrive at the restaurant at about the same time, thus no one would need to be waiting for anyone else to show-up. As you can imagine, there was some at times heated debate about which way was the fastest route to the restaurant. Some of the drivers thought that taking the freeway would be fastest, while others of the drivers tended to prefer using side streets since the freeway was likely to be clogged with commuter traffic.

After agreeing to go ahead and use the freeway (some grumbled about that, I assure you), we all got into our respective cars and started our informal car caravan on its way. Some of the drivers had obviously never tried to actually participate in a car caravan and they immediately zoomed ahead of everyone else, seemingly not having a care in the world about the rest of the cars in the caravan. Meanwhile, some of the drivers were admittedly the nervous Nellie kind of driver, and they began to fall way behind the rest of the pack.

Within just five to ten minutes of the caravan having gotten underway, we were no longer a "proper" caravan that could be considered of a line-of-sight nature. Some caravans try to keep all of the cars in a line-of-sight, meaning that each car that is a member of the caravan can see at least the car ahead of it that is also a part of the caravan. In our impromptu version, we had cars now that were stretched miles apart from each other and the caravan had become a somewhat disjointed and sporadic series of segments of cars.

Adding to the exasperation was the fact that when we each tried to get onto the freeway, by bad luck the specific on-ramp that we all were going to use was closed down due to an accident that had happened about an hour earlier. This completely disrupted the caravan. Some of the drivers opted to continue onward to the next freeway on-ramp and therefore kept to the approach of using the freeway. Other drivers decided that this was a sure sign that using side streets was the better idea (it certainly made them feel high-and-mighty about earlier stating that side streets would be best), and so those drivers decided to not use the freeway at all.

I guess it is a miracle that we all made it to the restaurant, though the timing of arrival was rather scattered. Fortunately, no one got lost and we all eventually arrived at the restaurant. Luckily, there wasn't anyone that had a car problem like say a flat tire, and there wasn't anyone that opted to abandon the quest (though I'm sure there were rather pointed discussions inside some of the cars about whether to just give up trying to get to the restaurant and instead call it a night).

A kind of funny thing happened during the caravan antics. I got a call on my cell phone from someone that had arrived late to the professional association meeting and he was perplexed as to why there was no one there. I explained that we had decided to adjourn the meeting and headed to the restaurant for dinner. He asked if it was Okay for him to head to the restaurant and he also mentioned that a few other late arrivers were also standing around trying to figure out what was going on. I told him they certainly were all welcome to come to the restaurant.

This then prompted another caravan!

I found out later on at dinner, once they arrived, they had done the same things we had done. They had first discussed whom was driving with whom. This involved some complicated deliberations as to car sizes and the number and sizes of the people involved. Though they had fewer participants, they nonetheless ended-up with several cars involved and it was a miniature version of our original caravan. They debated whether to use the freeway versus side streets. Once underway, their cars rather quickly lost line-of-sight of each other, just as had happened to us. They each also encountered the closed-off freeway on-ramp (I sheepishly realized that I probably should have mentioned that aspect). And so on.

What does this have to do with AI self-driving cars?

At the Cybernetic AI Self-Driving Car Institute, we are developing AI software for self-driving cars. One so-called "edge" problem for self-driving cars involves their participation in a car caravan.

I'd like to first clarify and introduce the notion that there are varying levels of AI self-driving cars. The topmost level is considered Level 5. A Level 5 self-driving car is one that is being driven by the AI and there is no human driver involved. For the design of Level 5 self-driving cars, the auto makers are even removing the gas pedal, brake pedal, and steering wheel, since those are contraptions used by human drivers. The Level 5 self-driving car is not being driven by a human and nor is there an expectation that a human driver will be present in the self-driving car. It's all on the shoulders of the AI to drive the car.

For self-driving cars less than a Level 5, there must be a human driver present in the car. The human driver is currently considered the responsible party for the acts of the car. The AI and the human driver are co-sharing the driving task. In spite of this co-sharing, the human is supposed to remain fully immersed into the driving task and be ready at all times to perform the driving task. I've repeatedly warned about the dangers of this co-sharing arrangement and predicted it will produce many untoward results.

Let's focus herein on the true Level 5 self-driving car. Much of the comments apply to the less than Level 5 self-driving cars too, but the fully autonomous AI self-driving car will receive the most attention in this discussion.

Here's the usual steps involved in the AI driving task:
- Sensor data collection and interpretation
- Sensor fusion
- Virtual world model updating
- AI action planning
- Car controls command issuance

Another key aspect of AI self-driving cars is that they will be driving on our roadways in the midst of human driven cars too. There are some pundits of AI self-driving cars that continually refer to a utopian world in which there are only AI self-driving cars on the public roads. Currently there are about 250+ million conventional cars in the United States alone, and those cars are not going to magically disappear or become true Level 5 AI self-driving cars overnight.

Indeed, the use of human driven cars will last for many years, likely many decades, and the advent of AI self-driving cars will occur while there are still human driven cars on the roads. This is a crucial point since this means that the AI of self-driving cars needs to be able to contend with not just other AI self-driving cars, but also contend with human driven cars. It is easy to envision a simplistic and rather unrealistic world in which all AI self-driving cars are politely interacting with each other and being civil about roadway interactions. That's not what is going to be happening for the foreseeable future. AI self-driving cars and human driven cars will need to be able to cope with each other.

Returning to the topic of car caravans, this notion of an AI self-driving car participating in a car caravan is considered by many auto makers and tech firms as an edge problem. An edge problem is a portion of a larger problem but an aspect that is considered at the edge or corner of what you are trying to solve. Right now, the auto makers and tech firms are focusing on getting an AI self-driving car to drive properly on our roadways. This is a priority focus devoted to having a single "independent" car doing driving and doing so without hitting or harming others. Dealing with packs of cars that are trying to caravan together is not a priority at this time.

We do care about car caravans and I offer herein some of the challenges and opportunities involved in adapting AI to be able to consider AI self-driving cars in a caravan mode.

First, there is the question of whether a human will instigate the utilization of a car caravan or whether the AI itself might do so.

In the case of the professional association meeting caravan, if we had AI self-driving cars, we could have presumably expressed to our AI self-driving cars that we wanted to get to the restaurant and that as much as possible we wanted to do so as a car caravan. In that case, assuming that the AI self-driving cars each had a module dealing with car caravans, the AI respective systems could have electronically communicated with each other and potentially determined the logistics of the caravan journey for us.

The communication amongst the AI self-driving cars would likely occur via V2V (vehicle-to-vehicle communications). An AI self-driving car would attempt to open an electronic dialogue with another AI self-driving car and invoke the car caravan module. This specialized module would then take on the role of an overseer for figuring out the caravan details. This would be done in a federated manner and not require that there be one centralized system manager routine per se.

During the planning of the route to the desired destination, the AI self-driving cars could also make use of V2I (vehicle-to-infrastructure) electronic communications. AI self-driving cars are intended to operate in conjunction with "smart" roadway infrastructure, which might include that a bridge might electronically beam out a message that it is not passable or that a local street emits a signal that it is torn-up for road repair and should be avoided. In the case of my story about the professional meeting caravan, it is conceivable that if there was V2I that using it might have alerted us that the freeway on-ramp was closed. In which case, the argument we had about using the freeway versus using side streets might have been more easily resolved.

Once an AI self-driving car caravan gets underway, the AI self-driving cars can continue to keep tabs on each other by continuing to use V2V. If a lead self-driving car got to the freeway on-ramp first and discovered it was closed and hadn't been alerted beforehand by any relevant V2I broadcasting about it, the lead self-driving car could alert the other AI's of the self-driving caravan of cars. The AI's would then in real-time rapidly deliberate about the rerouting of the caravan.

This form of AI self-driving cars sharing with each other about their surroundings during a driving journey is referred to as omnipresence.

The rerouting of a self-driving car caravan is a bit trickier than you might think. One aspect involves how close the self-driving cars in the caravan are supposed to stay with each other. This would be a parameter that could be set by those involved in the caravan. If you were doing a caravan with loved ones as part of a funeral procession, you might want the caravan to be very tightly woven together. If the caravan involves simply going to a restaurant for dinner, you might allow the AI to let the caravan stretch out.

I had mentioned that the caravan of AI self-driving cars could be initiated by a human. Another way to initiate a car caravan might be via the AI itself.

Suppose that you are heading to work for your morning commute. You work at the ABC Building in downtown and live in a city that is about 20 miles away from the downtown area. If you are willing to share your destination with other AI self-driving cars, here's what could happen.

Your AI self-driving car via V2V starts communicating with other AI self-driving cars. Specifically, the AI is trying to find out if there are other AI self-driving cars that are heading to the same downtown destination. If so, the AI of your self-driving car might suggest to other nearby AI self-driving cars that are also going to downtown that they proceed collectively as a car caravan. The AI self-driving cars would work in unison with each other, trying to generally aid each other in getting to the desired destination.

Please note that I am not saying that the AI self-driving cars would need to form a tightly woven pack. As mentioned earlier, a caravan does not necessarily need to consist of vehicles that are bumper to bumper with each other (that's platooning). Instead, these AI self-driving cars in the virtual car caravan would arrange to at times to be close to one another and at other times perhaps be at some distance of each other. They could also be warning each other about road traffic status, street repairs, and other infrastructure related aspects that might or might not also be available via V2I.

It could be that every day, you go to work pretty much the same way, and as such the self-driving car caravan might become a learned and practiced effort for this particular route. The first time you engage it, the caravan might be an impromptu version. Later on, it might become a common place caravan that has established itself and provides value in being used over and again. This might include using a blockchain for purposes of keeping a sustainable version of the caravan aspects.

Overall, the approach is that a human can potentially initiate the use of a car caravan, or the AI itself can propose that a car caravan be used. This does bring up though some quite serious issues of privacy and other related concerns that need to be considered.

If your AI self-driving car starts broadcasting to other AI self-driving cars your destination, this could be a loss of privacy on your part, plus it could be a potential risk factor if you are someone that others might want to target. A variant then on the destination indication could be that rather than a specific address being communicated, the destination might be an overall location such as downtown. This would reduce somewhat the loss of privacy and the risk factors.

Another aspect to this car caravan is whether you as a human want to participate in it or not. If you initiate it, presumably you want to participate in it. If the AI initiates it, you might not want to be a participant, thus it would be crucial that the AI would let you know about the potential of joining a car caravan and allow you the choice of whether to join into it or not.

From a ridesharing perspective, the use of car caravans could be a substantive boost toward trying to optimize the number of people and the number of self-driving cars needed for particular journeys. Suppose there are other people in your neighborhood that need to also get to downtown for work each day. Rather than each of them taking a car to get there, the use of the car caravans might reveal a type of car pooling that could be undertaken.

There might be "private" car caravans and there might be "public" car caravans.

In the case of the story about my colleagues going to dinner, we would have considered our car caravan to be a private one. Even if some other AI self-driving car made contact and requested to participate, we would have likely not wanted any other such cars to be in the caravan other than the ones we considered part of our group. In contrast, a public oriented car caravan might be open to any other AI self-driving car that wants to participate in the caravan effort.

Some AI self-driving cars might have a caravan module, and some might not. I say this because many people falsely seem to think that all AI systems for all of the different auto makers self-driving cars will be the same.

They will not be.

Each auto maker will have a distinct set of features available in their AI self-driving cars.

Over time, we'll likely see that most of the auto makers tend to gravitate toward having the same or similar features in their AI self-driving cars.

Even for an AI self-driving car that does not have the caravan module, if such a module is generally available and compatible with the rest of the AI system of that self-driving car, it could potentially be downloaded via the OTA (Over The Air) capability of the self-driving car.

OTA is a feature that most auto makers are including in their AI self-driving cars and allows for the self-driving car to electronically communicate with the cloud of the auto maker or tech firm.

Doing so allows the auto maker or tech firm to upload data from the self-driving car, along with being able to download and install new data and systems patches into the AI self-driving car. A module for being able to undertake car caravan processing could potentially be so installed via OTA.

Car caravans can be used in a wide variety of settings. You might be heading on vacation with some friends, all of whom are driving their own cars, and you perhaps want to caravan together while visiting numerous wilderness sites across the country and other exciting destinations.

Or, you might use a car caravan for getting to work or for undertaking dinners meetings with professional colleagues. Caravans also include the somber occasions of a funeral procession, along with the rather hectic motorcades of VIP's.

AI self-driving cars can and should be able to participate in car caravans. If there is a mix of human driven cars and AI self-driving cars for a particular caravan instance, it will admittedly be harder to carry on the caravan.

When the car caravan consists of solely AI self-driving cars, and assuming they are outfitted with the proper add-on module, the caravan can be a nearly seamless experience for any human occupants that are in the cars of the caravan. I don't want to though exclude human driven cars and so let's not necessarily refer to this as self-driving car caravans and for the moment keep it to the broader notion of car caravans.

Wouldn't want to seem discriminatory towards human drivers.

APPENDIX

APPENDIX A

TEACHING WITH THIS MATERIAL

The material in this book can be readily used either as a supplemental to other content for a class, or it can also be used as a core set of textbook material for a specialized class. Classes where this material is most likely used include any classes at the college or university level that want to augment the class by offering thought provoking and educational essays about AI and self-driving cars.

In particular, here are some aspects for class use:

o   Computer Science. Studying AI, autonomous vehicles, etc.

o   Business. Exploring technology and it adoption for business.

o   Sociology. Sociological views on the adoption and advancement of technology.

Specialized classes at the undergraduate and graduate level can also make use of this material.

For each chapter, consider whether you think the chapter provides material relevant to your course topic. There is plenty of opportunity to get the students thinking about the topic and force them to decide whether they agree or disagree with the points offered and positions taken. I would also encourage you to have the students do additional research beyond the chapter material presented (I provide next some suggested assignments they can do).

RESEARCH ASSIGNMENTS ON THESE TOPICS

Your students can find background material on these topics, doing so in various business and technical publications. I list below the top ranked AI related journals. For business publications, I would suggest the usual culprits such as the Harvard Business Review, Forbes, Fortune, WSJ, and the like.

Here are some suggestions of homework or projects that you could assign to students:

a) <u>Assignment for foundational AI research topic</u>: Research and prepare a paper and a presentation on a specific aspect of Deep AI, Machine Learning, ANN, etc. The paper should cite at least 3 reputable sources. Compare and contrast to what has been stated in this book.

b) <u>Assignment for the Self-Driving Car topic</u>: Research and prepare a paper and Self-Driving Cars. Cite at least 3 reputable sources and analyze the characterizations. Compare and contrast to what has been stated in this book.

c) <u>Assignment for a Business topic</u>: Research and prepare a paper and a presentation on businesses and advanced technology. What is hot, and what is not? Cite at least 3 reputable sources. Compare and contrast to the depictions in this book.

d) <u>Assignment to do a Startup</u>: Have the students prepare a paper about how they might startup a business in this realm. They must submit a sound Business Plan for the startup. They could also be asked to present their Business Plan and so should also have a presentation deck to coincide with it.

You can certainly adjust the aforementioned assignments to fit to your particular needs and the class structure. You'll notice that I ask for 3 reputable cited sources for the paper writing based assignments. I usually steer students toward "reputable" publications, since otherwise they will cite some oddball source that has no credentials other than that they happened to write something and post it onto the Internet. You can define "reputable" in whatever way you prefer, for example some faculty think Wikipedia is not reputable while others believe it is reputable and allow students to cite it.

The reason that I usually ask for at least 3 citations is that if the student only does one or two citations they usually settle on whatever they happened to find the fastest. By requiring three citations, it usually seems to force them to look around, explore, and end-up probably finding five or more, and then whittling it down to 3 that they will actually use.

I have not specified the length of their papers, and leave that to you to tell the students what you prefer. For each of those assignments, you could end-up with a short one to two pager, or you could do a dissertation length paper. Base the length on whatever best fits for your class, and the credit amount of the assignment within the context of the other grading metrics you'll be using for the class.

I mention in the assignments that they are to do a paper and prepare a presentation. I usually try to get students to present their work. This is a good practice for what they will do in the business world. Most of the time, they will be required to prepare an analysis and present it. If you don't have the class time or inclination to have the students present, then you can of course cut out the aspect of them putting together a presentation.

If you want to point students toward highly ranked journals in AI, here's a list of the top journals as reported by *various citation counts sources* (this list changes year to year):

- o Communications of the ACM
- o Artificial Intelligence
- o Cognitive Science
- o IEEE Transactions on Pattern Analysis and Machine Intelligence
- o Foundations and Trends in Machine Learning
- o Journal of Memory and Language
- o Cognitive Psychology
- o Neural Networks
- o IEEE Transactions on Neural Networks and Learning Systems
- o IEEE Intelligent Systems
- o Knowledge-based Systems

GUIDE TO USING THE CHAPTERS

For each of the chapters, I provide next some various ways to use the chapter material. You can assign the tasks as individual homework assignments, or the tasks can be used with team projects for the class. You can easily layout a series of assignments, such as indicating that the students are to do item "a" below for say Chapter 1, then "b" for the next chapter of the book, and so on.

a) What is the main point of the chapter and describe in your own words the significance of the topic,

b) Identify at least two aspects in the chapter that you agree with, and support your concurrence by providing at least one other outside researched item as support; make sure to explain your basis for disagreeing with the aspects,

c) Identify at least two aspects in the chapter that you disagree with, and support your disagreement by providing at least one other outside researched item as support; make sure to explain your basis for disagreeing with the aspects,

d) Find an aspect that was not covered in the chapter, doing so by conducting outside research, and then explain how that aspect ties into the chapter and what significance it brings to the topic,

e) Interview a specialist in industry about the topic of the chapter, collect from them their thoughts and opinions, and readdress the chapter by citing your source and how they compared and contrasted to the material,

f) Interview a relevant academic professor or researcher in a college or university about the topic of the chapter, collect from them their thoughts and opinions, and readdress the chapter by citing your source and how they compared and contrasted to the material,

g) Try to update a chapter by finding out the latest on the topic, and ascertain whether the issue or topic has now been solved or whether it is still being addressed, explain what you come up with.

The above are all ways in which you can get the students of your class involved in considering the material of a given chapter. You could mix things up by having one of those above assignments per each week, covering the chapters over the course of the semester or quarter.

As a reminder, here are the chapters of the book and you can select whichever chapters you find most valued for your particular class:

Lance B. Eliot

Companion Book By This Author

Advances in AI and Autonomous Vehicles: Cybernetic Self-Driving Cars

Practical Advances in Artificial Intelligence (AI) and Machine Learning
by
Dr. Lance B. Eliot, MBA, PhD

This title is available via Amazon and other book sellers

<u>Companion Book By This Author</u>

Self-Driving Cars:
"The Mother of All AI Projects"

by Dr. Lance B. Eliot, MBA, PhD

This title is available via Amazon and other book sellers

This title is available via Amazon and other book sellers

**New Advances in AI Autonomous
Driverless Cars Self-Driving Cars**

by Dr. Lance B. Eliot, MBA, PhD

This title is available via Amazon and other book sellers

Companion Book By This Author

Introduction to
Driverless Self-Driving Cars

by Dr. Lance B. Eliot, MBA, PhD

This title is available via Amazon and other book sellers

Companion Book By This Author

Autonomous Vehicle Driverless Self-Driving Cars and Artificial Intelligence

by Dr. Lance B. Eliot, MBA, PhD

<u>Chapter Title</u>

This title is available via Amazon and other book sellers

Companion Book By This Author

Transformative Artificial Intelligence Driverless Self-Driving Cars

by Dr. Lance B. Eliot, MBA, PhD

This title is available via Amazon and other book sellers

Companion Book By This Author

Disruptive Artificial Intelligence and Driverless Self-Driving Cars

by Dr. Lance B. Eliot, MBA, PhD

Chapter Title

This title is available via Amazon and other book sellers

Companion Book By This Author

State-of-the-Art
AI Driverless Self-Driving Cars

by Dr. Lance B. Eliot, MBA, PhD

This title is available via Amazon and other book sellers

Lance B. Eliot

<u>Companion Book By This Author</u>

***Top Trends in
AI Self-Driving Cars***

by Dr. Lance B. Eliot, MBA, PhD

<u>Chapter Title</u>

This title is available via Amazon and other book sellers

Lance B. Eliot

216

Companion Book By This Author

AI Innovations and Self-Driving Cars

by Dr. Lance B. Eliot, MBA, PhD

This title is available via Amazon and other book sellers

Companion Book By This Author

Crucial Advances for AI Self-Driving Cars

by Dr. Lance B. Eliot, MBA, PhD

Chapter Title

This title is available via Amazon and other book sellers

<u>Companion Book By This Author</u>

***Sociotechnical Insights and
AI Driverless Cars***

by Dr. Lance B. Eliot, MBA, PhD

<u>Chapter Title</u>

This title is available via Amazon and other book sellers

Companion Book By This Author

Pioneering Advances for
AI Driverless Cars

by Dr. Lance B. Eliot, MBA, PhD

Chapter Title

This title is available via Amazon and other book sellers

Companion Book By This Author

Leading Edge Trends for AI Driverless Cars

by Dr. Lance B. Eliot, MBA, PhD

Chapter Title

This title is available via Amazon and other book sellers

Companion Book By This Author

The Cutting Edge of AI Autonomous Cars

by Dr. Lance B. Eliot, MBA, PhD

<u>Chapter Title</u>

This title is available via Amazon and other book sellers

Lance B. Eliot

Companion Book By This Author

The Next Wave of
AI Self-Driving Cars

by Dr. Lance B. Eliot, MBA, PhD

Chapter Title

This title is available via Amazon and other book sellers

Companion Book By This Author

Revolutionary Innovations of AI Self-Driving Cars

by Dr. Lance B. Eliot, MBA, PhD

Chapter Title

This title is available via Amazon and other book sellers

Companion Book By This Author

AI Self-Driving Cars
Breakthroughs
by Dr. Lance B. Eliot, MBA, PhD

Chapter Title

This title is available via Amazon and other book sellers

ABOUT THE AUTHOR

Dr. Lance B. Eliot, MBA, PhD is the CEO of Techbruim, Inc. and Executive Director of the Cybernetic AI Self-Driving Car Institute, and has over twenty years of industry experience including serving as a corporate officer in a billion dollar firm and was a partner in a major executive services firm. He is also a serial entrepreneur having founded, ran, and sold several high-tech related businesses. He previously hosted the popular radio show *Technotrends* that was also available on American Airlines flights via their in-flight audio program. Author or co-author of a dozen books and over 400 articles, he has made appearances on CNN, and has been a frequent speaker at industry conferences.

A former professor at the University of Southern California (USC), he founded and led an innovative research lab on Artificial Intelligence in Business. Known as the "AI Insider" his writings on AI advances and trends has been widely read and cited. He also previously served on the faculty of the University of California Los Angeles (UCLA), and was a visiting professor at other major universities. He was elected to the International Board of the Society for Information Management (SIM), a prestigious association of over 3,000 high-tech executives worldwide.

He has performed extensive community service, including serving as Senior Science Adviser to the Vice Chair of the Congressional Committee on Science & Technology. He has served on the Board of the OC Science & Engineering Fair (OCSEF), where he is also has been a Grand Sweepstakes judge, and likewise served as a judge for the Intel International SEF (ISEF). He served as the Vice Chair of the Association for Computing Machinery (ACM) Chapter, a prestigious association of computer scientists. Dr. Eliot has been a shark tank judge for the USC Mark Stevens Center for Innovation on start-up pitch competitions, and served as a mentor for several incubators and accelerators in Silicon Valley and Silicon Beach. He served on several Boards and Committees at USC, including having served on the Marshall Alumni Association (MAA) Board in Southern California.

Dr. Eliot holds a PhD from USC, MBA, and Bachelor's in Computer Science, and earned the CDP, CCP, CSP, CDE, and CISA certifications. Born and raised in Southern California, and having traveled and lived internationally, he enjoys scuba diving, surfing, and sailing.

ADDENDUM

AI Self-Driving Cars Breakthroughs

Practical Advances in Artificial Intelligence (AI) and Machine Learning

By
Dr. Lance B. Eliot, MBA, PhD

———

For supplemental materials of this book, visit:

www.ai-selfdriving-cars.guru

For special orders of this book, contact:

LBE Press Publishing

Email: LBE.Press.Publishing@gmail.com